2009

Merry Christmas, Dad!

♡ Dave + Suz xoxo

WHAT'S COOKING IN NEW ENGLAND?

a taste from farms to seaside bistros all over new england

A collection of New England recipes from farms

to seaside bistros and all that's in between

Diane Perry Gardner
Photography by Chris Devlin Brown
Design by Stephanie Magriz and Tammy Vaz

Published by

ISBN: 978-0-9824836-0-2

Welcome

The hardest part about moving to Connecticut 20 years ago was leaving my home of Lake City, South Carolina. Yes, I was excited to share this adventure with my new husband, but I felt that I was literally ripping the roots of my life out of the comforts of everything I had… my family, my friends, my home. How was I going to transplant myself and all my nostalgic Southern sentiments into the austere Yankee culture that awaited me?

As I slowly infused my days with the quaint lifestyle that endears New England to natives and visitors alike, I discovered that I could just as easily call Connecticut "home" as I had so recently done with South Carolina. I could shamelessly cling to the cliché "Home is where the heart is", and find solace in knowing that my roots hadn't truly been ripped away from my Southern beginnings…. I had just taken a cutting from them, and transplanted them into a new environment, where they flourished amidst new-found friends, the joyful arrival of my children, and our daily involvement in our community.

One of my earliest observances as a new "Nutmegger" was the difference in food. I grew up on fried chicken with rice and gravy (my favorite), and country-style steak smothered in onions and gravy. And the plate was always piled high with fresh vegetables. Of course I had to save room for the best to come… coconut cake or pecan pie. Always the perfect ending to a lazy Sunday afternoon. Yet I soon discovered the delights of New England fare… a hearty stew on winter's day, the salty-sweet heaven of a lobster roll on a toasted hot dog bun, the tangy bite of a warm cranberry quick bread. Meal time at our home became a sumptuous combination of culinary cultures.

Over the years, I collected dozens of recipes from friends and neighbors, and what I found so intriguing was that many of them came with stories, passed down from generation to generation, filled with love. It's a wonderful way to nourish a family, and keep us connected to our past. When I decided to write this book, my travels through Connecticut, Rhode Island, Massachusetts, New Hampshire, Vermont, and Maine proved that there is no shortage of unusual tales to explain the history of a recipe:

When asked about her mother's home baked beans (page 161), Judy Mager of Westbrook, Connecticut, said that this is the oldest family recipe she has, and she's been making it for 43 years! Before Judy could cook, her mother made these beans for 50 years!!

Lita Lynfesty Beal of Beals Island, Maine, calls her recipe for bread pudding "By Guess or By Gory" (page 289). I questioned the "gory", thinking it was supposed to be "glory", but was quickly corrected. "Gory" is a local Maine term meaning and as the recipe reads, a tad of this and a pinch of that! This has been passed down from generation to generation! This is definitely my favorite type of recipe.

Scott Woodford of Madison, Connecticut, shared his horror story of being a part of the "clean your plate club". With a family of six, it was always "waste not, want not" era! Scott's father would take him fishing for blue fish. "We would fill the damn boat with the sharp-toothed cousins of piranha... we could not give them away.... Even the Indians used them in their corn fields for fertilizer... so I cringed when Friday night came in late winter. As my father would say, there is no wasting perfectly good food no matter how bad the oily, freezer-burned fish tasted!!! Scott has now taken to the idea of trying to feed his kids a character-building meal and he calls it "Not My Dad's fish cakes"!! (page 188)

As I heard more stories, I recognized how connected the cooks were to their recipes and their New England heritage. And while I considered myself fully integrated into the New England culture after 20 years, I realized that my Southern roots continue to hold me firmly to my own heritage. That is why I decided to include some of my favorite dishes from my personal recipe box, many cards stained and ragged from years of creating savory connections from my "south of the Mason-Dixon line" upbringing to my Yankee family. The common thread with all of the recipes in this book is the love for cooking and the joy of sharing it with people who appreciate great food, whether nestled into a quaint corner table of a romantic mountain-side inn or gathered around the kitchen table marred by years of school projects and family dinners.

So, I encourage you to enjoy my hybrid of North and South, and cherish the connections that you and your family may create because of it.

Diane

About the Author

With her books in more than 250 book stores, gift shops, boutiques, and restaurants spanning from northern Maine to New York City, it's nearly impossible to comprehend that Diane Gardner's cookbooks evolved from her need to escape boredom.

As a full-time, stay-at-home mom, Diane has immersed herself into the joys of raising a family in the quaint shoreline town of Madison, Connecticut. Married to Bill, an executive in the Industrial industry, for more than 20 years, Diane's lifestyle carries the same crazy schedule as most families with three busy children. Getting the kids to school, carpooling for basketball and tennis practice, monitoring homework and attending business functions with her husband.

Jesse, Ty, and Halle know how lucky they are to have a mom like Diane. On any given school morning, they know they can shout down their individual breakfast requests to the kitchen, whether it's Eggs Benedict, Chocolate Chip Pancakes, or a simple egg & cheese sandwich, and Diane will have it served as they all discuss the day's upcoming activities. And all three teens enjoy the perks of hanging out at home with their friends. A weekend at the Gardner home can be comprised of legions of teens relaxing in the kitchen, munching on hand-dipped strawberries in chocolate fondue. Diane sees food as an opportunity to get to know her children (and their friends), an experience that both she and Bill cherish.

Adventure vacations and international travel have provided many opportunities for the Gardner family to discover new interests and unusual foods. Over the years, Diane has had the privilege to dine around the globe and experience hundreds of culinary creations. Yet, her favorite 'restaurant' is her own kitchen, where she can perfect recipes, experiment with new ingredients, and then settle into the family room for a moderately competitive game of Set-Back or Presidenté with family and friends.

A full schedule and a wonderful family life wasn't enough to keep Diane fully engaged, and she began her venture into the world of creating cookbooks. Meeting with chefs and cooks, scouting out epicurean markets, testing new recipes, managing distribution orders, and scheduling book signings now fill her already-busy calendar. The concept of boredom is a distant memory.

Diane thrives on her passion for cooking, and embraces any opportunity she can to share her experience, techniques, and tips that will encourage everyone to enjoy creating meals that are memorable and fun. Diane's videos can be found on YouTube.com, and her website (www.whatscookinginnewengland.com) boasts her latest recipes. Diane is also available for cooking demonstrations and event consultations. Slumber party catering, however, is not available, with exceptions made only for Bill, Jesse, Ty, and Halle!

Table of Contents

Photo on Left:
Location provided by Marisa and Steve Drew at their home "Rockbound", Sachem Head, Guilford, CT.
Table styling provided by Maggie's of Madison, Madison, CT.
Lanterns provided by Schofield Historic Lighting, Ivoryton, CT.
Stemware, silverware, and dinnerware courtesy of Juliska.

starting flavors

susan's herb butter with mussels

bear's bleu cheese shrimp

crab and scallop cakes

portuguese littlenecks

antipasto squares

sausage calzones

crabmeat dip

maine stone crab

baked brie

crab artichoke and spinach dip

steamed mussels

savory salsa cheesecake

leek and goat cheese tart

cornmeal crust and
goat cheese flatbread

starting flavors

mushrooms parmigiana in filo

feta with sundried tomatoes

cocktail meatballs

mary's spinach bread

coffee's crab cakes

holiday meatballs

spring rolls

maine mussels

pan-fried new england
wild mushrooms

steak tartare

grilled shrimp

shrimp strudel

lamb chops

susan's herb butter with mussels

Shared by Susan Warner, Nantucket Clambake Company, Nantucket, Massachusetts

I created this recipe when I catered one of my very first clambakes. Using seasonal fresh herbs from my garden, I created a very flavorful butter.

The ingredient that makes this herb butter different from others is the use of sorrel. Although I use this butter to accompany native Nantucket mussels as part of my island clambake dinner, this butter works really well with littleneck clams.

HERB BUTTER:

1/2 pound salted butter	1/2 cup sorrel, chopped
1 small onion, diced	1 tablespoon oregano, chopped
1/2 cup garlic, minced	
1/2 cup basil, chopped	1/2 cup fresh lemon juice
1/4 cup parsley, chopped	3–4 cups canned plum or fresh tomatoes, chopped
1/4 cup tarragon, chopped, leaves stripped off stems	freshly ground pepper, to taste

INSTRUCTIONS:

In a medium saucepan, melt 1/4 pound of butter over medium-high heat. Add onion and sauté until transparent. Add garlic and lightly sauté. Melt in remaining butter. Add herbs and lemon juice. Add chopped tomatoes. If using fresh tomatoes, pulverize in food processor. Season with pepper to taste. Cook for another 3–4 minutes. Do not boil.

MUSSELS:

2 pounds mussels, cleaned	1/2 cup dry white wine

INSTRUCTIONS:

In a large saucepan, cook mussels over high heat with the white wine. Bring to a simmer. Cook only a few minutes until mussels have opened, stirring frequently to ensure they are evenly cooked. Discard any mussels that have not opened.

Pour herb butter over mussels and toss. Serve mussels family style in a large serving bowl, alongside a basket of sliced French baguette, great for soaking up all that delicious butter.

bear's bleu cheese shrimp

Shared by Katie Gildersleeve, Stamford, Connecticut

2¹/₂ pounds shrimp, shelled and cleaned

2 lemons, thinly sliced

1 teaspoon Old Bay seasoning

1 cup tarragon vinegar

¹/₃ cup olive oil

¹/₃ tablespoon nutmeg

¹/₃ tablespoon whole cloves

2 small onions, thinly sliced

¹/₂ teaspoon Polaner's garlic, minced

¹/₂ pound bleu cheese, crumbled

¹/₂ cup roasted red peppers, chopped

¹/₂ cup green peppers, chopped

20 bay leaves

salt, to taste

pepper, to taste

paprika, to taste

Tabasco sauce, to taste

INSTRUCTIONS:

Cook shrimp until pink with half the lemon slices and Bay seasoning. Let shrimp cool. Starting with the vinegar, mix remaining ingredients together; pour over cooled shrimp. Cover and refrigerate overnight.

Before serving, remove bay leaves and arrange whole ones on a salad plate. Place 5 shrimp on top, then artistically place some lemon slices and onion slices on shrimp and spoon bleu cheese marinade over shrimp. Serves 25 hors d'oeuvres, 10–12 appetizers, 6–8 luncheons.

crab and scallop cakes
with chipotle aioli

*Shared by Esau Crosby, Executive Chef
at Solo Bistro Bistro, Bath, Maine*

CAKES:

3	ounces butter	2	teaspoons salt
4	ounces sweet onion, minced	1	teaspoon ground black pepper
6	ounces green and red peppers, minced	1	pound scallops, chopped medium fine
1	teaspoon ground chipotle pepper	1	pound fresh crabmeat
		2–4	ounces fine bread crumbs

INSTRUCTIONS:

Preheat oven to 425 degrees. Brown butter in oven safe pan; add vegetables and seasonings. Sauté until soft. Set aside to cool in bowl. Chop and add the scallops and crabmeat to cooled vegetable mixture. Mix well. Add enough bread crumbs to make the mixture firm enough to handle. Scoop to make desired size of cake and sauté in butter, turning once. Finish by placing pan in oven for 10–15 minutes at 325 degrees.

CHIPOTLE AIOLI:

1	cloves garlic, finely chopped	3	tablespoons ketchup
3	cans chipotle peppers, in juice, finely chopped	2	limes, zested
		3	large eggs
1	teaspoon salt	2	limes, juiced
1	teaspoon pepper	3	cups olive oil
			parsley, for garnish

INSTRUCTIONS:

Finely chop garlic and peppers in food processor. Add the seasonings, ketchup and lime zest. Scrape down sides and puree as fine as possible. Place eggs in processor and add lime juice. Slowly drizzle olive oil until completely blended. Recommended to make this a day in advance.

To serve, place crab and scallop cakes on small appetizer plate, dollop with chipotle aioli and garnish with fresh parsley. Serves 8 as an appetizer or 4 as an entree.

portuguese littlenecks

**Shared by Brick Alley Pub and Restaurant,
Newport, Rhode Island**

*This award-winning appetizer is the perfect start to any meal
or add some linguine and make it a hearty dinner! This recipe
has been featured in Bon Appétit several times. The Brick
Alley Pub is a must visit if you are in Newport.*

1 pound chouriço, casings removed and crumbled (Spanish chorizo may be substituted)

2 large white onions, halved, thinly cut crosswise, 1/3 inch thick slices

2 large green bell peppers, cut into 1/3 inch thick slices

2 8 ounce bottles clam juice

1 cup dry white wine

1/4 teaspoon dried red pepper, crushed (more if sausage is mild)

32 littleneck clams, about 5 pounds, scrubbed

3/4 cup fresh cilantro, chopped, divided

1 red bell pepper, finely chopped

1 lemon, cut into 8 wedges

INSTRUCTIONS:

Heat large pot over medium-high heat. Add first 3 ingredients to pot; sauté until vegetables are tender and sausage is brown, stirring frequently and breaking up sausage with back of fork, about 10 minutes. Add clam juice, wine, crushed red pepper; bring to a boil. Reduce heat to medium; simmer 3 minutes. Add clams; cover and cook until clams open, about 8 minutes. Discard any clams that do not open. Stir in 1/2 cup cilantro.

Transfer mixture to a large bowl. Top with 1/4 cup cilantro and red bell pepper. Garnish with lemon wedges and serve with crusty bread. Serves 4.

antipasto squares

Shared by Dottie Starwarky, Westbrook, Connecticut

2	tubes crescent rolls	1/4	pound pepperoni, thinly sliced
1/4	pound Swiss cheese, thinly sliced	1	large jar sweet roasted peppers
1/4	pound ham, thinly sliced	3	eggs
1/4	pound provolone cheese, thinly sliced	1/4	cup Parmesan cheese, grated
1/4	pound salami, thinly sliced		

INSTRUCTIONS:

Roll out 1 tube of crescent rolls and fit into the bottom of a 13 x 9 greased pan. Layer in Swiss cheese, ham, provolone cheese, salami, pepperoni and red peppers, in that order, on top of the crescent roll.

Beat eggs with Parmesan cheese and pour on top of layers. Save some to brush on top. Roll out second crescent roll and place on egg mixture. Brush top with remaining egg mixture. Cover with foil and bake for 30 minutes at 350 degrees. Uncover, prick top with fork and bake for another 15–20 minutes until top is golden brown. Let sit 15 minutes. Cool and cut into squares.

sausage calzones

Shared by Mary Jensen, Contuit, Massachusetts

1	pound hot turkey or chicken Italian sausage	1	package fresh pizza dough
6	ounces turkey pepperoni, sliced	12	ounces reduced fat mozzarella cheese, shredded

INSTRUCTIONS:

Remove sausage from casing and sauté over low heat until no longer pink. Break up in pieces and drain off fat. Set aside. Stack pepperoni slices and cut in quarters.

Shape dough into an oval and cut in half. Roll each half in a cylinder shape on floured cutting board. Should be 14 inches long and 5 inches wide ... this takes time.

Place drained, cooled sausage into a wooden bowl and use a chopper to remove any chunks. Mix in mozzarella cheese and pepperoni thoroughly. Place handfuls onto rolled out dough in equal amounts. Pull dough sides together and use water or egg wash to enclose mixture. Overlap the ends.

Place calzones on a greased cookie sheet and bake in a preheated oven at 350 degrees for 25 minutes. Makes 2 small calzones.

crabmeat dip

Shared by Ruth Carver, Beals Island, Maine

*My husband, Guy, is a lobster fisherman and when
he brings the offshore crabs in from his traps,
I cook them and pick them out for this dip.*

1	8-ounce package cream cheese, softened	1	tablespoon ketchup
1/3	cup mayonnaise	3	teaspoons onion, minced
		1/2	pound crabmeat

INSTRUCTIONS:

Whip with a mixer all of the ingredients except for the crabmeat until
well blended and smooth.

Gently fold in crabmeat and put in the fridge to cool.

maine stone crab
with tobiko, avocado and sesame

Shared by Black Point Inn, Prouts Neck, Scarborough, Maine

1	pound Maine stone crabmeat, picked and checked for shell pieces	1	tablespoon white sesame seeds, toasted, plus some for garnish
2	tablespoons mayonnaise	1	ripe Hass avocado
1	teaspoon lemon zest	2	teaspoons fresh lemon juice
2	tablespoons orange tobiko		salt, to taste
4	tablespoons chives, chopped		pepper, to taste
1	tablespoon aged sherry vinegar		

INSTRUCTIONS:

Combine all ingredients except avocado and lemon juice and press into four 2¼ inch x 2 inch deep pastry cutters set onto appetizer plates. Cube the avocado and mix with lemon juice, salt and pepper. Remove pastry cutters for a perfectly shaped mound of crabmeat. Top each with avocado mixture and garnish with toasted sesame seeds.

baked brie

Shared by Mimi Franz, Madison, Connecticut

2	pounds brie	¼	teaspoon allspice
3	cups fresh cranberries	¼	teaspoon cardamom
¾	cup light brown sugar	¼	teaspoon ground cloves
½	cup dried currants	¼	teaspoon ginger
¾	cup water	¼	teaspoon dried mustard

INSTRUCTIONS:

Let brie come to room temperature and cut off top rind. Mix together everything except the brie and cook over medium heat until the cranberries start to pop. Take off stove, let sit. Scoop into the brie approximately ½ inch. Load the chutney on top. Bake at 350 degrees for 12–15 minutes. Let stand for 15 minutes after it comes out of oven. Serve with wheat crackers.

crab artichoke and spinach dip

Shared by Bills Seafood, Westbrook, Connecticut

3	cans artichoke hearts	3	ounces Parmesan cheese
6	ounces sour cream	5	ounces spinach
6	ounces mayonnaise		Tabasco sauce, to taste
3	ounces cream cheese		white pepper, to taste
6	ounces mozzarella cheese, shredded	8	ounces crabmeat

INSTRUCTIONS:

Drain artichokes and squeeze out the liquid. Add all ingredients to pan except crab. Turn heat on low and cook for 15–20 minutes. Puree until smooth. Drain crabmeat, squeeze out the liquid and add crab to mixture. Stir gently and serve warm with chips, crackers or vegetables.

steamed mussels
cozze al vino bianco

Shared by Sardella's Restaurant, Newport, Rhode Island

A great start to any meal! A favorite in Newport.

40 medium mussels	2 cloves garlic, finely chopped
½ cup clam broth	salt, to taste
½ cup white wine	pepper, to taste
3 ounces olive oil	red pepper flakes, to taste
½ medium white onion, chopped	

INSTRUCTIONS:

In a large pot at high heat, add mussels, clam broth, wine, olive oil, onion and garlic. Season with salt, pepper and red pepper flakes. Cover pot and bring to a boil. When all mussels have opened, remove from heat and place mussels in a large bowl; cover with sauce. Discard any mussels that did not open. Serve with crusty Italian bread for dipping. Serves 4.

savory salsa cheesecake

Shared by Lorraine King, Hampton, New Hampshire

3	8-ounce packages cream cheese, softened	1	4-ounce can green chilies, diced
1	cup sour cream	½	cup Manchego or Monterey Jack cheese, shredded
½	cup roasted red peppers, chopped		pineapple-mango salsa (I use Appledore Cove)
1	teaspoon chili powder		
3	eggs		
2	tablespoons all purpose flour		

INSTRUCTIONS:

Beat cream cheese and sour cream at medium speed. Add the pepper pieces and chili powder; beat until just blended. Add the eggs and flour and beat until thoroughly combined. Do not overbeat or cheesecake will crack. Stir in by hand the green chilies and shredded cheese.

Coat an 8-inch springform pan with cooking spray. Pour cheese mixture, spreading evenly, into pan. Place the cheesecake on a rack or on an upside down ramekin set in the bottom of a 5-quart electric slow cooker. Carefully pour 1–2 cups hot water around the sides of the pan on the bottom of the slow cooker.

Cover and cook on high heat about 2 hours or until set. Turn off the slow cooker. With paper towels, blot any excess moisture on top of cheesecake. Run a knife around edge of cheesecake. Remove lid and let stand in cooker for about 1 hour to cool.

Remove pan from slow cooker and cool the cheesecake to lukewarm. Cover and chill for 3–4 hours. Just before serving, remove the springform sides of the pan and put cheesecake on serving platter. Top with salsa. Serve with chips. Makes 1 appetizer cheesecake for 10 or more servings.

leek and goat cheese tart

Shared by Jason Sobocinski, Caseus Fromagerie and Bistro, New Haven, Connecticut

PATE BRISÉE:

2 cups flour	1/2 cup cold water
1/2 pound butter	egg wash, 1 egg mixed with 1 tablespoon milk
pinch salt	

FILLING:

4 leeks, white and light green only	salt, to taste
	pepper, to taste
1 tablespoon olive oil	1/2 pound goat cheese*, crumbled
1 tablespoon butter	

CUSTARD:

1 cup cream	salt, to taste
1 whole egg	pepper, to taste
1 egg yolk	

INSTRUCTIONS:

Preheat oven to 350 degrees. Make the pate brisée by combining flour, butter and salt in an electric mixing bowl and mixing until the butter is crumbled into small pieces. Slowly add only enough water to make the dough come together. Cover and let rest for 20 minutes in the refrigerator.

Wash and cut leeks into small pieces. Combine oil and butter in a sauté pan over medium heat. Lightly sauté leeks until tender and fragrant. Season with salt and pepper. Remove to clean bowl and cool.

Roll out the pate brisée. Fit into individual tart rings on a baking sheet. Let rest for 20 minutes in the refrigerator.

Whisk together the cream, egg and yolk. Season to taste with salt and pepper. Fill each tart with sautéed leeks and crumbles of goat cheese. Add custard mixture until 1/8 inch from the top of the tart. Brush the tart shell with the egg wash. Bake for 15–20 minutes or until golden brown and custard has set. Serve warm or room temperature. Makes 8 individual tarts.

*See reference page 307

cornmeal crust and goat cheese flatbread

Shared by Fat Toad Farm, Brookfield, Vermont

We grow Calais flint corn every summer and I am always looking for creative ways to use cornmeal besides cornbread. This is an excellent winter meal for us because we use frozen pesto from the summer, local flour, our own cornmeal, sundried tomatoes, sausage from our pigs and our goat cheese.

CRUST:

1/8 teaspoon sugar

1 1/4 cups warm water

2 1/4 teaspoons active dry yeast

1 1/2 cups unbleached white flour

1 cup whole wheat flour

2/3 cup cornmeal

1 teaspoon salt

3 1/2 tablespoons extra virgin olive oil

TOPPINGS:

6 ounces pesto

6 ounces chèvre*

6 ounces mozzarella cheese, shredded

or

6 ounces sundried tomato basil chèvre*

4 ounces mozzarella cheese, shredded

1/2 pound sausage or hamburger, cooked and drained

INSTRUCTIONS:

Mix sugar, warm water and yeast together. Wait 5 minutes. In large bowl mix together white flour, 1/2 cup whole wheat flour, cornmeal and salt. Stir in water mixture and olive oil until just combined. On floured surface knead dough for 10 minutes adding the other 1/2 cup whole wheat flour to create a shiny, moist but not wet dough.

Oil a large bowl. Put dough in bowl covering all sides with oil. Cover with plastic wrap and leave in a warm place to rise for an hour.

Preheat oven to 500 degrees. Once dough has doubled in size, roll out on a lightly floured surface. This dough is enough for 1 large thick crust pizza or 2 small thin crust pizzas. Oil the top of the pizza pan and put dough on. Rub a thin layer of oil all over the top of the crust. Sprinkle crust with a pinch of salt. Let rest for 15 minutes.

Cook crust on bottom rack for 5 minutes.

Spread ingredients in any combination on the pizza crust and cook on bottom rack for 5 more minutes. Move to the middle rack for 3–4 minutes or until golden brown. *See reference page 307

mushrooms parmigiana in filo

Shared by Dorothy Vaz, Glastonbury, Connecticut

This recipe was given to me by a friend. I have made this for Christmas for over 20 years. I make so many appetizers for Christmas; however, this is one of my family's favorites, and there are never any leftovers.

12 ounces mushrooms, finely chopped	3 tablespoons Parmesan cheese, grated
1/4 cup green pepper, finely chopped	1 tablespoon snipped parsley
1 clove garlic, minced	1/2 teaspoon salt
1 medium onion, finely chopped	1/4 teaspoon dried oregano dash pepper
2 ounces sausage or pepperoni, diced	1/3 cup chicken broth
2 tablespoons butter	1 pound filo leaves, thawed
1/2 cup crackers, finely crushed	1/2 pound sweet butter, melted

INSTRUCTIONS:

Cook mushrooms, pepper, garlic, onion and pepperoni in butter until vegetables are tender, but not brown. Add cracker crumbs, cheese, parsley, salt, oregano and pepper; mix well. Stir in chicken broth. Unroll filo leaves and cut in halves. Keep filo covered with damp towel; this keeps the filo from drying out.

Take 1 piece of filo and brush with butter. Place 1 tablespoon of filling in the center of the filo about 1 inch from the edge. Fold sides over center and roll up filo, securely tucking in all ends. Brush finished rolls with additional butter. Place on baking sheet at 350 degrees for about 15 minutes. Makes 40 pieces.

mary's spinach bread

Shared by Mary Dangelo, Narragansett, Rhode Island

*I just love stuffed breads. Here is my version of spinach
bread, which is very easy and tastes so good!*

1	pound bread dough from pizza shop or grocery store
2–3	tablespoons olive oil
1	small box chopped spinach, thawed and strained
1/2	cup pepperoni, chopped
2	cloves garlic, chopped
1/2	teaspoon red pepper flakes
	salt, to taste
	pepper, to taste
1	cup mozzarella cheese, grated

INSTRUCTIONS:

Roll out dough into 12 x 8 rectangle and set aside.

In fry pan, add olive oil and sauté spinach, pepperoni, garlic and red
pepper flakes. Season with salt and pepper. Cook about 5–8 minutes,
until it is hot and well combined. Let cool for a few minutes, then lay
spinach down the center of the dough. Sprinkle with cheese. Starting on
one end, roll the dough as if it were a jelly roll. Place onto cookie sheet,
seam down, and bake at 375 degrees for 25 minutes.

The steam that is created by putting 1/2 cup water in an ovenproof cup
will help give the bread a crispy crust. Bake until golden brown. Slice
and enjoy hot or at room temperature.

coffee's country market crab cakes
with cajun aioli

Shared by Coffee's Country Market, Old Lyme, Connecticut

CRAB CAKES:

1 pound cooked lump crabmeat

1 cup fine dry bread crumbs

1 tablespoon Dijon mustard

1 teaspoon Worcestershire sauce

2 teaspoons Old Bay seasoning

3 tablespoons fresh cilantro, finely chopped

1 large egg

2 tablespoons mayonnaise

2 teaspoons fresh lemon juice

zest of 1 lemon

1 small yellow pepper, seeded and finely chopped

1 small red pepper, seeded and finely chopped

1 large shallot, finely chopped

5 tablespoons vegetable oil

freshly ground black pepper, to taste

INSTRUCTIONS:

Combine crabmeat and bread crumbs in a medium bowl and set aside. In another bowl combine wet ingredients: mustard, Worcestershire, Old Bay, cilantro, egg, mayonnaise, lemon juice and zest. Stir until well combined. Set aside. In a skillet lightly sauté, about 3–5 minutes, peppers and shallot in 1 tablespoon vegetable oil. Cool and combine with crabmeat mixture. Combine crab with wet ingredients. Season with pepper to taste. Using fingers, shape crab into ¾ inch thick, half dollar size rounds.

Heat remaining vegetable oil in skillet over medium heat. Working in small batches, cook crab cakes until golden brown on bottom, 1 minute. Turn and repeat. Transfer crab cakes to parchment lined sheet pan and bake for 10 minutes or until heated through.

Serve with Cajun aioli. This can also be served with Asian slaw for a wonderful lunch or dinner. *See page 156 for Asian Slaw.*

CAJUN AIOLI:

1 cup mayonnaise

5 scallions, cleaned and finely chopped

zest of 1 lime

juice of 1 lime

2–3 tablespoons Cajun spice mix

INSTRUCTIONS:

Combine all ingredients and mix well.

holiday meatballs

Shared by Christopher's by the Bay Bed and Breakfast, Provincetown, Massachusetts

1 package precooked
frozen meatballs

1/4 teaspoon dry mustard

1 tablespoon white vinegar

1 8-ounce can cranberry
sauce, jellied

3/4 cup ketchup

INSTRUCTIONS:

In a slow cooker, combine all ingredients except the meatballs. Turn on high and stir. When the mixture is heated and saucy, add the frozen meatballs and cook on low for 3–4 hours, covered. Stir occasionally so that the meatballs become well coated with sauce. Enjoy.

spring rolls

Shared by Nesia Baker, Clinton, Connecticut

1	pound ground pork		salt, to taste
2	carrots, shredded		pepper, to taste
2	celery stalks, shredded	1	package egg roll
3–4	cloves garlic, minced		wrappers
2	scallions, chopped		chili sauce

INSTRUCTIONS:

In a large heavy skillet, brown ground pork over medium heat until cooked through. Add carrots, celery, garlic, scallions, salt and pepper and continue to cook until veggies soften. Place ⅔ tablespoon of pork mixture in each egg roll wrapper, roll until edges come together and bake in a 350 degree oven until crispy brown. Or pan fry until crispy. Serve with a bowl of chili sauce for dipping. To add spice to egg roll, mix chili sauce into filling to taste. Can substitute pork with chicken, shrimp or beef.

maine mussels
with fresh orange and rosemary

*Shared by Esau Crosby, Executive Chef
at Solo Bistro Bistro, Bath, Maine*

2	tablespoons olive oil	1	orange, quartered
1	tablespoon garlic, minced	½	cup white wine
1	tablespoon fresh ginger, chopped	2	sprigs fresh rosemary
1	pound fresh Maine mussels, cleaned	4	tablespoons butter
			salt, to taste
			pepper, taste

INSTRUCTIONS:

In a hot sauté pan, heat the oil. Add garlic and ginger and cook until garlic browns. Add mussels and toss to coat. Squeeze orange segments into pan. Add wine, rosemary sprigs and butter. Season to taste with salt and pepper. Cover and cook until the mussels open. Serves 2–4.

pan-fried new england wild mushrooms
with vermont cheddar and thyme butter

*Shared by Matthew Jennings, La Laiterie at Farmstead,
Providence, Rhode Island*

3	cups wild New England mushrooms, wiped clean and stalks trimmed		kosher salt, to taste
			black pepper, to taste
2	tablespoons olive oil	1	cup heavy cream
1	"knob" unsalted butter	2	tablespoons fresh chives, sliced
1	tablespoon fresh thyme leaves	1/3	cup Vermont cheddar*, grated

INSTRUCTIONS:

Cut the mushrooms in thin slices, using "chicken of the woods," "hen of the woods" or "boletes." Heat oil in a heavy bottomed skillet. Add the mushrooms and sauté for 3 minutes or until the mushrooms are golden brown and very tender.

Add the butter and thyme to the pan and season with kosher salt and black pepper to taste. Once the butter starts to melt, stir in the cream and chives. Cook for another 2–3 minutes until slightly reduced, stirring occasionally. Divide up the mushroom mixture among warmed, wide rimmed bowls and sprinkle the aged cheddar on top. Serve immediately with grilled, crusty bread. Serves 4.

See reference page 307

steak tartare
dante style
Shared by Andrea Dante, MIREPOIX Catering, Guilford, Connecticut

Every Sunday afternoon whether it was just the four of us or my parents were entertaining guests, the Dante family would serve my father's take on this classic French dish. My sister, Laura, and I would stand tiptoed atop milk crates assisting my father, Chris, as his pint-sized sous chefs, hoping to sneak a caper "dividend" or two!

As a career chef today, I still serve this favorite appetizer to friends and clients alike. The trick is using great meat from a local butcher or gourmet grocery store.

3 egg yolks	1/4 cup watercress, chopped
1 tablespoon mustard	2 teaspoons Worcestershire sauce
4 anchovy fillets, minced	
1/4 cup GOOD olive oil	2 pounds butcher ground sirloin
1/2 cup Spanish onion, finely chopped	kosher salt, to taste
1/2 cup small capers, rinsed and drained	black pepper, to taste

INSTRUCTIONS:

In a large bowl, whisk yolks, mustard and anchovies together. Continue whisking, slowly drizzle in oil to emulsify. Add the next 4 ingredients; stir once to combine. Using hands or wooden spoon, add meat and mix well. Season to taste with salt and pepper. Chill for 20 minutes or more. Can be made a day ahead.

To serve, use the bowl as a mold or mound the tartare onto a plate and shape as desired. Surround with toast points or favorite crackers. Leftovers make terrific flavorful hamburgers.

grilled shrimp

Shared by Teresa and Art Swanson, Manchester, Connecticut

*This is a dish that is made to be eaten with your fingers.
The trick is to suck all the liquid from the nooks and crannies
of the shrimp before peeling it. Group dipping in the
sauce is encouraged.*

1	pound black tiger shrimp, with shell on, split and deveined
6	cloves fresh garlic, pressed
4–6	tablespoons white wine Worcestershire sauce
1	heaping tablespoon capers
$1/2$	teaspoon red pepper flakes
1	tablespoon red hot sauce or Habanero hot sauce, to taste
$1/4$–$1/3$	cup olive oil
$1/8$	cup white wine (Chardonnay or Gewürztraminer is best)
$1/4$	cup white wine, for deglazing
	Hungarian paprika
	salt, to taste
	pepper, to taste

INSTRUCTIONS:

Mix all ingredients, except extra $1/4$ cup wine, in a bowl. Heat skillet with enough olive oil to cover the bottom of the pan. Bring to high heat. Carefully spoon shrimp mixture into pan. Oil will splatter, so be cautious. Cook shrimp on one side for 1–2 minutes, then flip. When shrimp are pink, transfer only the shrimp to a large, flat bowl. Do not transfer liquid. Add approximately $1/4$ cup wine to liquid and deglaze at a high heat to a gravy-like thickness, stirring constantly. Pour over shrimp and serve immediately with lots of slices of thick, crusty bread to soak up the sauce.

shrimp strudel

Shared by Susan Morgan, Killingworth, Connecticut

1 1/2	cups Muenster cheese, shredded	1/4–1/2	teaspoon salt
1	cup cooked shrimp, chopped	1/8	teaspoon pepper
1/4	cup green onions, thinly sliced	1	8-ounce package crescent rolls, refrigerated
2	eggs	1	tablespoon butter, melted

INSTRUCTIONS:

In a large bowl, stir together cheese, shrimp, onions, eggs, salt and pepper; set aside. Unroll crescent roll dough onto a lightly floured surface. Pinch together perforations on both sides of dough. Fold in half crosswise and with lightly floured pin, roll out to 14 x 19 inch rectangle. Brush with butter.

Spread cheese-shrimp mixture in 2-inch strip along the long edge of the dough; roll up like a jelly roll. Firmly pinch seams and ends together. Carefully lift roll onto ungreased cookie sheet. Bake in preheated oven at 400 degrees for 25 minutes or until golden brown. Cool on rack for 20 minutes. With sharp knife cut in 1/2 inch slices. Makes 28 appetizer servings.

lamb chops

Shared by Diane Gardner, Madison, Connecticut

*This recipe was in my first book and everyone loved it,
so here it is again!!*

1   package Australian lamb
    chops, individually sliced

    fresh rosemary, chopped

    kosher salt

    freshly ground black
    pepper

    olive oil

    whole sprigs rosemary,
    for garnish

INSTRUCTIONS:

Place chops on a baking sheet. Mix rosemary, kosher salt and pepper
together. Add olive oil to form a paste. Rub each chop on both sides.
Grill over high heat for about 2 minutes on each side. Serve immediatcly
and garnish with fresh sprigs of rosemary.

breakfast, brunch & breads

strawberry scones

pecan pie mini-muffins

portuguese sailor sandwich

french toast casserole

crispy hash browns

portuguese bread–folar

christmas sausage apple ring

blueberry pancakes

broccoli cornbread

apple peach bread

lemon glazed blueberry cupcakes

oat scones

quick brunch quiche

portuguese biscoitos

rich butterhorn rolls

banana walnut stuffed french toast

downeast cranberry nut bread

cranberry scones

breakfast, brunch & breads

strawberry scones

Shared by Simon's Marketplace, Chester, Connecticut

Simon's has emerged as one of the hubs of Chester's eclectic community ... a daily haven for artists, professionals and families alike. An amazing selection for breakfast and lunch!

3	cups all purpose flour		2	cups fresh strawberries, chopped
1/3	cup sugar			
1	teaspoon baking soda		1	cup buttermilk
1	tablespoon baking powder			extra sugar, for sprinkling
1/2	teaspoon salt			butter, melted, for brushing top
1/2	pound unsalted butter			

INSTRUCTIONS:

Mix flour, sugar, baking soda, baking powder and salt together. Cube butter into 1/2 inch squares and mix into flour by hand or food processor until a crumbly meal begins to form.

Add chopped strawberries and mix by hand. Add buttermilk and gently mix with a rubber spatula or wooden spoon until dough starts to come together.

Lightly flour work surface area and quickly knead dough only enough to hold together, perhaps 2–5 turns. DO NOT OVER KNEAD, as this tends to make scones flat. Shape the dough into a rectangle, about 8 inches long and 4 inches wide. Cut in half to make 2 rectangles. Roll out each rectangle about 1/2 inch thick and shape. Brush each rectangle with butter and sprinkle generously with sugar. Again cut each rectangle in half, making 2 squares; cut squares into 4 triangles each. Place on baking sheet with parchment paper. Bake at 350 degrees for about 10 minutes or until edges turn golden brown.

pecan pie mini-muffins

Shared by Brenda Martin, Charleston, South Carolina

1 cup brown sugar, packed	²/₃ cup butter, melted (no substitutes)
¹/₂ cup all purpose flour	
1 cup pecans, chopped	2 eggs, beaten

INSTRUCTIONS:

In a bowl, combine brown sugar, flour and pecans; set aside. Combine butter and eggs; mix well. Stir into flour mixture until just moistened. Fill greased and floured or paperlined muffin cups two thirds full. Bake at 350 degrees for 20–25 minutes or until muffins test done. Remove immediately to cool on wire rack. Yields about 2¹/₂ dozen.

portuguese sailor sandwich

Shared by Brick Alley Pub and Restaurant, Newport, Rhode Island

A favorite brunch sandwich!

2	pieces Portuguese sweet bread, thickly sliced	2	chouriço patties
		2	eggs
2	slices cheddar cheese		butter or oil, for grilling

INSTRUCTIONS:

Grill bread until golden brown. Cover bread with cheddar cheese while it is on the grill or fry pan to melt. Broil or grill chouriço patties. Fry eggs. Break yolks for a less runny sandwich. Place eggs and patties between sweet bread slices and serve with a little fresh fruit. Serves 1.

french toast casserole

Shared by Dottie Starwarky, Westbrook, Connecticut

1	loaf French or Italian bread	1	tablespoon vanilla
8	large eggs	2	tablespoons butter, cut in small pieces
3	cups milk		cinnamon, for sprinkling on top before baking
4	teaspoons sugar		
3/4	teaspoon salt		maple syrup, heated

INSTRUCTIONS:

Grease a 13 x 9 pan. Cut bread into 1 inch pieces and layer on bottom of pan. Beat eggs with remaining ingredients, except butter, and pour over bread in pan. Spread the butter pieces on top of casserole. Cover with foil and refrigerate overnight. Add cinnamon and bake uncovered at 350 degrees for 45–50 minutes before serving. Top with hot maple syrup and serve with bacon or sausage. Serves 6.

crispy hash browns

Shared by Dana Maciel, Seekonk, Massachusetts

This is a great recipe… I make it for breakfast, lunch, dinner, potluck and just about anything else. Everyone loves it and there is never any left.

1 can cream of chicken soup	1/2 cup butter, melted
2 pounds frozen hash browns	1 cup sour cream
	salt, to taste
10 ounces cheddar cheese, shredded	1/2 cup milk
	1/2 cup onion, chopped

TOPPING:

3/4 cup Ritz crackers	1/4 cup butter, melted

INSTRUCTIONS:

Combine all ingredients; do not thaw the hash browns. Place in a greased 9 x 13 pan. Combine Ritz crackers with butter and sprinkle over top of mixture. Bake for 1 hour at 350 degrees. This can be prepared a day in advance and baked the day of serving.

portuguese bread
folar

Shared by Tony Vaz, Glastonbury, Connecticut

Folar is a Portuguese Easter tradition that has been passed on for generations. My sister-in-law, Hilda, taught me to make this bread, and I have made it for my family over the past 40 years.

3	packages yeast	2	tablespoons olive oil
1	cup luke warm water	1	pound linguiça (Portuguese sausage)
2	dozen eggs		
6–7	pounds flour	1	pound ham, bacon, pepperoni
2	sticks butter		

INSTRUCTIONS:

Mix yeast with water. Add flour, mix eggs into flour. Mix butter and olive oil. Mix all together; punch dough to help rise. Then slap dough down.

Let rise for 2–4 hours; the dough is ready when it rises up in the mixing bowl. Cover with towels and put dough bowl in warm place. Now sauté ham a little to rid of fat and then cut linguiça, ham, bacon and pepperoni.

Split dough for separate loaves; then stretch out dough sides, put meat in center and fold dough to the center to shape loaves. Mix 2 eggs for egg wash, then brush on the top of each loaf. Spray pans, then place shaped loaves into separate pans. Cook at 350 degrees for 30–35 minutes. Makes 4 large plus 4 small loaves.

christmas sausage apple ring

Shared by Bill Suhr, Champlain Orchards, Shoreham, Vermont

*For decades this recipe has been a Suhr/Anders
Christmas morning tradition.*

1 large onion, about ½ cup	1½ cups bread crumbs (can be packaged Pepperidge Farm, seasoned)
2 eggs	
½ cup parsley, chopped	½ cup milk
2 pounds leanest, mild bulk sausage (Jimmy Dean sausage with ham)	1–2 cups tart apples, chopped
	grind or two of pepper

INSTRUCTIONS:

Blend onion, eggs and parsley in blender. In a large bowl, combine all ingredients, mixing well with hands. With cling wrap, line the bottom of a 6 cup ring mold or a large Bundt pan for a double portion. Press sausage mixture lightly into mold; turn out into a square of foil on a flat rack in a roasting pan; puncture the foil in the middle of the ring. Bake at 350 degrees for 1 hour. Drain off all fat. Use a suction-baster to remove fat in the center of the ring if it accumulates while baking.

blueberry pancakes

Shared by a local in Camden, Maine

When you make these pancakes drop the blueberries onto the pancakes once they are on the griddle.

1	cup unbleached flour	¹/₄	cup sour cream
3	teaspoons baking powder	1	teaspoon vanilla
¹/₂	teaspoon salt	3	tablespoons unsalted
2	tablespoons sugar		butter, melted
1	large egg	¹/₂	cup Maine blueberries
1	cup milk or half and half		

INSTRUCTIONS:

Sift together the flour, baking powder, salt and sugar in a mixing bowl. In separate bowl beat the egg, milk, sour cream and vanilla. Pour over the dry ingredients and mix well. Add the melted butter. Heat a lightly greased skillet or cast iron fry pan over medium heat. When it is hot, pour a ¹/₄ cup of batter on skillet and then drop blueberries onto the batter. Cook until lightly browned on both sides. Makes approximately fifteen 4-inch pancakes.

broccoli cornbread

Shared by Loretta Tallevast, Lake City, South Carolina

1	box Jiffy cornbread mix	1	small onion, chopped
4	eggs, beaten	1	box frozen broccoli, thawed and well drained
1	stick margarine, melted		
6	ounces cottage cheese		

INSTRUCTIONS:

Stir together Jiffy, eggs and margarine. Stir in cottage cheese and then add onion and broccoli. Pour into a greased 9 x 13 baking dish and bake at 400 degrees for 25 minutes or until done. Serves 8–10.

apple peach bread

Shared by Noquochoke Orchards, Westport, Massachusetts

1½ cups brown sugar, packed	1 teaspoon vanilla
⅔ cup oil	2½ cups flour
1 egg	1 teaspoon baking soda
1 cup sour milk (add 1 tablespoon vinegar to milk)	1 cup peaches, diced
	1 cup apples, diced
	½ cup nuts, chopped

INSTRUCTIONS:

Combine sugar and oil. Beat in egg, milk and vanilla. Mix well. Sift flour and baking soda into the egg mixture; beat for 2 minutes. Fold in peaches, apples and nuts. Pour into 2 greased and floured loaf pans. Bake at 325 degrees for 40–45 minutes. Bananas or pears can be substituted for peaches.

lemon glazed blueberry cupcakes

Shared by Ruth Carver, Beals Island, Maine

I only use Maine wild blueberries for this recipe.
They are plentiful during August and September;
after that I use my frozen ones. The glaze adds
a nice crunchy top for these wicked good cupcakes.

CUPCAKES:

1/2 cup unsalted butter, softened	2 1/4 cups all purpose flour
1 1/2 cups granulated sugar	4 teaspoons baking powder
2 large eggs	1/2 teaspoon salt
1/2 teaspoon pure vanilla extract	1 cup milk
	1 1/4 cups Maine wild blueberries

GLAZE:

3 tablespoons water	1/2 teaspoon lemon zest, grated
1 cup confectioners' sugar	
2 teaspoons lemon juice	

INSTRUCTIONS:

Preheat oven to 375 degrees. Butter 24 muffin cups or use paper muffin cups. Beat butter and sugar until smooth. Add eggs and vanilla and blend well. In a separate bowl, sift 2 cups of flour with the baking powder and salt. Toss berries in remaining 1/4 cup of flour.

On medium speed add flour to butter mixture, alternating with 1 cup of milk. Fold in the berries. Spoon batter into muffin cups and bake for 15 minutes. Meanwhile, whisk the water with remaining 3 ingredients for the glaze until smooth, thick but pourable. After cupcakes have baked for 15 minutes, take out of the oven and spoon 1 tablespoon of glaze over each. Return to oven and bake until golden brown on top and a skewer comes out clean. Immediately run a small knife around each cake to loosen any glaze and unmold onto a wire rack.

oat scones

Shared by The Governor's House in Hyde Park, Vermont

These scones are served as part of our full English afternoon tea. I make them flat and heart shaped and serve them with clotted cream and strawberry jam. I usually serve them warm out of the oven, but they also freeze well.

³/₄	cup oat flour	³/₄	teaspoon salt
1	tablespoon baking powder	¹/₄	cup cold butter
3	tablespoons maple sugar	¹/₂	cup buttermilk
1¹/₄	cups flour	1	egg, room temperature, beaten

INSTRUCTIONS:

Mix all dry ingredients. Cut in butter. Add milk to beaten egg and pour over dry mixture. Fold together lightly and form a ball. Roll out on floured board to about ³/₄ inch thick. Cut and place on ungreased cookie sheet. Bake in 400 degree oven until lightly brown.

quick brunch quiche

Shared by Kathleen Campbell, Cornucopia Wine and Cheese Market, Stratham, New Hampshire

8	slices ciabatta Tuscan bread, cubed	1	pound bacon, cooked and crumbled
1/2	pound Australian cheddar cheese*, grated	8	eggs
1/2	pound Cave aged Gruyère cheese*, grated	2	cups whole milk
3	green onions, diced	1 1/2	cups half and half
		2	teaspoons Worcestershire sauce
		1	teaspoon dry mustard

INSTRUCTIONS:

Butter 3 quart casserole dish. Place cubed bread in bottom of dish. Layer with cheese, then onions and bacon. Beat eggs; add milk, half and half and seasonings. Pour over bread mixture. Cover. Let stand overnight in refrigerator. Bake at 325 degrees for 1 hour. Serves 10.

See reference page 307

portuguese biscoitos

Shared by Aunt Rose, Somerset, Massachusetts

This is from my dear aunt Rose's collection of Portuguese recipes in her head, passed from generation to generation. We all go to my aunt's house and watch her bake these since she's got the touch and Lord only knows what else she does to them that is not included in the recipe.... You know when you bake something from your head and heart rather than from a recipe; you just do it instinctively! But all in all... they are good with coffee. Enjoy.

8	eggs	½	teaspoon baking powder
3	cups sugar	2	sticks unsalted butter, room temperature
4	teaspoons vanilla extract		
4	cups flour	1	tablespoon canola oil, if needed
4	small boxes Jiffy corn muffin mix		

INSTRUCTIONS:

In a small bowl, blend eggs and sugar very well; add vanilla. In another, larger bowl, combine flour with Jiffy mix and baking powder, break up butter into flour mixture and egg mixture and knead well. Put in refrigerator until cold and hard. Set oven to 425 degrees. Take a small amount of dough, roll it out and form a ring. If dough is dry, add a little canola oil. Place on cookie sheet and bake for about 7–8 minutes or until golden brown. Let cool on tray for 45 seconds and transfer to a wire rack to cool.

rich butterhorn rolls

Shared by Mary Dangelo, Narragansett, Rhode Island

Many, many years ago my husband and I bought a new freezer, maybe 50 years ago, and inside the freezer was a small paper cookbook. I found this recipe inside that book and thought I would try it. It was very good and I've made these rolls for every Christmas, Thanksgiving and Easter after that. I am almost 87 years old and I guess that is a lot of rolls!

1	cup milk	3	eggs, slightly beaten
¹/₂	cup shortening	4	cups all purpose flour
1	package cake yeast		butter, melted, for
¹/₂	cup sugar		brushing top of rolls
1	teaspoon salt		

INSTRUCTIONS:

Scald milk and then remove from heat. Add shortening. Combine yeast and sugar and add to lukewarm milk mixture. Then mix in salt, eggs and flour. Let rise until double in bulk, about 2 to 3 hours. Place on floured board, divide into 3 sections and roll each section into a circle about ¹/₂ inch thick. Brush with melted butter. Cut 20 pie-shaped wedges. Beginning at round edge, roll each wedge and place it on greased pan with the pointed end underneath. Brush top with melted butter. Let rise again until double in bulk. Bake 15 minutes in a preheated oven of 400 degrees. Makes 5 dozen small rolls.

banana walnut stuffed french toast

Shared by Mountain Village Farm B & B,
Kingfield, Maine

8	tablespoons butter	6	large eggs
3	bananas, peeled and chopped	1	teaspoon vanilla
½	cup walnuts, chopped	1	cup sugar
2	tablespoons brown sugar	12	slices Texas toast or other thick sandwich bread
1	teaspoon cinnamon		maple syrup
½	cup brandy		

INSTRUCTIONS:

Melt 1 tablespoon butter in small saucepan. Cook the bananas and walnuts until the bananas are very soft, 3–4 minutes. Add brown sugar, cinnamon and brandy and cook for 5 more minutes. Set aside to cool.

With a wire whisk, whip together eggs, vanilla and sugar in large bowl. Spread ¼ inch of banana mixture on 6 slices of bread. Top with remaining bread. Soak sandwiches in egg mixture for 5 minutes, turning halfway through. Melt the remaining 7 tablespoons butter in 2 large sauté pans. Sauté the sandwiches until golden brown on both sides. Serve with maple syrup. Serves 4–6.

downeast cranberry nut bread

Shared by Community of Christ Church, Jonesport, Maine

Cranberries are native to Downeast Maine. We buy them in Machias at the health food store. I believe they come from Jonesboro, and they are bright red and beautiful and so tart. This is a perfect bread for the Thanksgiving table.

2½ cups all purpose flour

1¼ cups granulated sugar

2 teaspoons baking powder

½ teaspoon baking soda

½ teaspoon salt

1 large egg

½ cup orange juice

¼ cup lemon juice

2 tablespoons unsalted butter, melted

1½ cups cranberries, coarsely chopped (do not overchop)

¾ cup walnuts or pecans, chopped

INSTRUCTIONS:

Grease medium size loaf pan. Sift or whisk together flour, sugar, baking powder, baking soda and salt. In separate bowl whisk the egg, orange and lemon juices and melted butter. Pour liquid ingredients into the dry ingredients and stir gently but thoroughly to blend. Fold in the cranberries and nuts. Preheat oven to 350 degrees. Pour batter into pan and bake for 1 hour and 15 minutes or until skewer comes out clean. Cool in pan 15 minutes and turn out onto rack.

cranberry scones

**Shared by Alyssa Gladchun, The Coffee Grinder,
Newport, Rhode Island**

*Voted the Best Coffee in town, The Coffee Grinder is the
place to go for breakfast or lunch! Located at the end of
Bannister's Wharf, overlooking Newport Harbor.*

3/4	pound butter, softened	1	teaspoon baking soda
1/2-3/4	cup sugar	1/2	quart buttermilk
6	cups flour	2	cups dried cranberries
1 1/2	tablespoons, plus 1/2 teaspoon baking powder		

INSTRUCTIONS:

Cream together the butter, sugar, flour, baking powder and baking soda.
Add buttermilk and mix just to blend. You don't want to blend too well.
Fold in cranberries. Bake at 425 degrees for 10-15 minutes. Makes
approximately 15 scones.

yankee red flannel hash

**Shared by Jackie Arbuckle, May Farm Bed and Breakfast,
Stowe, Vermont**

*I am not sure if people outside of New England are familiar
with using beets in hash, but we grew up with this! This is
delicious served with fried or scrambled eggs. Guest choice.*

1/3	cup onion, finely chopped	3	cups cooked potatoes, finely chopped
1/4	cup canola or olive oil	1	pound canned or fresh beets, cooked
1 1/2	cups cooked corned beef, finely chopped	1/3	cup milk
		1/2	teaspoon salt

INSTRUCTIONS:

In a skillet, cook onion in hot oil until tender, but not brown. Lightly
toss together with remaining ingredients. Spread evenly over bottom of
skillet. Cook over medium heat until the bottom of hash is brown and
crusty. Serves 4.

corner cafe
portobello scrambler

Shared by Bill Wooton, Corner Cafe, Newport, Rhode Island

A local favorite!!

3 eggs	1 ounce cheddar cheese, shredded
1/2 ounce half and half	pinch dried parsley
1 medium portobello cap	pinch dried thyme
1 ounce frozen spinach, thawed	pinch dried chives
1 ounce white onion, chopped	2 ounces hollandaise sauce, from powdered mix

INSTRUCTIONS:

Beat eggs and half and half together; reserve. Grill portobello cap; reserve. Heat a greased 8-inch skillet on high flame. Sauté spinach and onion in skillet. When soft, add egg mixture and scramble. Just before completely scrambled, add cheddar and herbs; finish scrambling. Place portobello cap on plate, top with scrambled mixture and top off with hollandaise sauce. Sprinkle with additional herbs and serve with home fries and toast!

southern biscuits

Shared by Loretta Tallevast, Lake City, South Carolina

2   cups self-rising flour   1   cup whole milk
²/₃ cup Crisco shortening

INSTRUCTIONS:

Sift flour and then measure. Using a fork, cut Crisco into flour. Slowly add milk and stir. Put on floured board and knead until dough is not sticky. Roll out with a rolling pin, about ¹/₂ inch thick. Cut with biscuit cutter or form into round balls and press with hands to form a biscuit. Bake at 400 degrees until golden brown, about 12–15 minutes. Serves 8.

cranberry pecan streusel coffeecake

Share by Cape Cod Cranberry Growers' Association, Cape Cod, Massachusetts

STREUSEL:

1 1/4 cups whole wheat or regular pastry flour

1/2 cup light brown sugar, packed

1 teaspoon ground cinnamon

6 tablespoons unsalted butter, softened

1 cup pecans, chopped

COFFEECAKE:

1 1/4 cups whole wheat pastry flour, sifted

3/4 cup sugar

1/2 cup unsalted butter, softened

1 teaspoon baking powder

1/4 teaspoon baking soda

1/4 teaspoon salt

1/2 teaspoon lemon zest

1/2 teaspoon vanilla extract

1/4 teaspoon ground cinnamon

1/4 cup buttermilk

2 eggs

1 cup fresh or frozen cranberries, chopped

INSTRUCTIONS:

To make the streusel, combine the flour, sugar and cinnamon in a small bowl. Rub the softened butter into the flour mixture until it holds together when squeezed. Gently mix in the pecans; set aside.

For the coffeecake, combine the flour, sugar, butter, baking powder, baking soda, salt, flavorings and buttermilk in a mixing bowl. Mix on low speed for 1 minute, scrape the bowl and beat for another 30 seconds, then scrape the bowl again.

Slowly add the eggs, 1 at a time, combining well after each addition. Scrape the bowl after each egg is added. Mix on medium speed for 1 minute. Gently fold in the cranberries by hand.

Grease an 8 x 8 pan and place about half of the batter in the pan. Smooth it out evenly with a small spatula. Spread one third of the streusel topping over the coffeecake batter. Lace the remaining coffeecake batter on top of the streusel and gently smooth out to the edges of the pan. Top with the remaining streusel.

Bake at 350 degrees in a preheated oven for 45–50 minutes. Allow the cake to cool in pan.

coffee grinder chocolate biscotti

Shared by Alyssa Gladchun, The Coffee Grinder, Newport, Rhode Island

Located at the end of the pier on Bannister's Wharf, overlooking Newport Harbor, the best view and the very best Chocolate Biscotti!!

1	pound butter, softened	2 tablespoons baking powder
3	cups sugar	splash vanilla
8	eggs	chocolate chunks, to taste
7	cups flour, approximately	

INSTRUCTIONS:

Blend butter and sugar together, slowly add one egg at time and mix well. Add baking powder to flour and mix well with wet mixture. Add splash of vanilla and fold in chocolate chunks to taste. May substitute with almonds. Bake at 350 degrees until firm to touch, remove from oven, slice with a serrated knife and put back in for a few minutes. Makes 2 loaves.

sour cream biscuits

Shared by Loretta Tallevast, Lake City, South Carolina

¹/₂ pound butter	1 cup sour cream
2 cups self-rising flour, sifted	

INSTRUCTIONS:

Mix butter and flour by hand. Stir in sour cream. Drop 2 teaspoons of mixture into small muffin tins. Bake for 30 minutes until brown. To freeze, bake for 20 minutes, cool and then freeze. Thaw when ready to use and bake for 10 minutes. Makes 36 small biscuits.

breakfast parfait

Shared by Diane Gardner, Madison, Connecticut

1 cup low fat yogurt	1 banana, sliced
¼ cup blueberries	½ cup granola
¼ cup raspberries	

INSTRUCTIONS:

In a parfait glass, making layers, add a little yogurt, berries, bananas and granola. Continue to layer and finish with granola. Easy and delicious.

apple popovers

Shared by Mavis Munger, Champlain Orchards, Shoreham, Vermont

Delicious for breakfast with lots of butter or jam. Serve with pork or as a dessert with maple syrup. Mavis has worked at Champlain Orchards for many years, back to when it was called Larrabee's Point Orchard!

1	cup flour	2	eggs
1/2	teaspoon salt	2	apples, peeled, sliced
1	cup milk		

INSTRUCTIONS:

Preheat oven to 425 degrees. Thoroughly butter popover cups or large muffin pans. Dust with flour so the batter can climb the edges. Mix all ingredients well. Pour each muffin cup half full. Place 1 or 2 apple slices into the center of batter. Bake in hot oven for 35–40 minutes. To keep popovers from collapsing, make sure to bake till crusty. After removing from oven, poke each popover with a knife to allow steam to escape. Run knife around edge to remove popovers.

herb bread

Shared by The Governor's House in Hyde Park, Vermont

This is served as part of a basket of homemade bread for dinner, but sliced thin it makes a lovely ham tea sandwich!

1	tablespoon yeast	2	tablespoons Parmesan cheese, grated
3	cups warm water	2	tablespoons Herbes de Provence
½	cup honey	1	tablespoon basil, chopped
8	cups bread flour, approximately	¼	cup olive oil
1	teaspoon salt		
1	tablespoon extra virgin olive oil		

INSTRUCTIONS:

Dissolve yeast in water. Add honey and about 4 cups flour. Mix well and let this sponge rise until it's light and bubbly. Stir in salt and olive oil. Knead in as much flour as needed to make firm dough. Let rise until double. Punch down and let rise again. Divide dough into 2–3 balls and roll into flat rectangles. Paint liberally with extra virgin olive oil. Sprinkle cheese and herbs and roll jelly fashion. Let rise a bit in well greased bread pans and slit the tops. Bake at 350 degrees until golden and pulling away from the sides of pans, about 40 minutes for 3 large loaves.

martin house blueberry scones

**Shared by Skye Schuyler, Innkeeper, Martin House Inn,
Nantucket, Massachusetts**

*Martin House is a year-round escape
into the heart of Nantucket Island.*

4 cups flour	$^1/_2$ teaspoon baking soda
1 cup sugar	$^1/_2$ pound unsalted butter
2 teaspoons baking powder	2 cups fresh blueberries
$^1/_2$ teaspoon salt	2 cups heavy cream

INSTRUCTIONS:

Mix flour, sugar, baking powder, salt and baking soda together. Add butter and mix with hands. Next pour in blueberries and heavy cream and mix with hands. Dump on floured surface and roll into ball, mixture should be smooth. Roll into rectangle, fold into thirds, roll and fold again into thirds. Roll final time and put into 9-inch round cake pans. Pre-cut before baking into slices. Bake until light brown, approximately 20–25 minutes. Makes 2 round 9-inch pans. Serves 16.

pumpkin bread

**Shared by Megan Bresnahan, Innkeeper,
Scargo Manor, Dennis, Massachusetts**

$1^1/_2$	cups sugar	$^1/_2$	teaspoon nutmeg
$1^2/_3$	cups flour	$^1/_2$	cup canned or fresh
1	teaspoon salt		pumpkin
1	teaspoon baking soda	$^1/_2$	cup oil
$^1/_2$	teaspoon ginger	$^1/_2$	cup water
$^1/_2$	teaspoon cinnamon	2	eggs
$^1/_2$	teaspoon allspice		walnuts, optional
$^1/_2$	teaspoon ground cloves		

INSTRUCTIONS:

Mix together the first 9 dry ingredients. Set aside. Mix together the
pumpkin, oil, water and eggs and add to the flour mixture. Add nuts if
desired. Bake in greased 9 x 5 loaf pan for 35–40 minutes at 350 degrees.

cinnamon french toast soufflé

Shared by Sue Zaccagnino, Madison, Connecticut

1	large loaf cinnamon bread, cubed	3/4	cup maple syrup
12	ounces cream cheese, softened	10	eggs
6	ounces butter, softened	3	cups half and half
			cinnamon sugar
			powdered sugar

INSTRUCTIONS:

Place cubed bread in a well buttered 13 x 9 pan. Mix cream cheese, butter and 1/4 cup of syrup until smooth. Spread over top of bread, leaving holes through which to pour the egg mixture. Beat eggs, half and half and remaining maple syrup. Pour over bread and sprinkle with cinnamon sugar. Cover and refrigerate overnight. Uncover and bake for 50–55 minutes at 350 degrees. Cut into squares and sprinkle with powdered sugar. Serves 8.

popovers

Shared by Judy Brawn, Dexter, Maine

3	large eggs	3	tablespoons butter, melted
1	cup milk	1/3	teaspoon salt
1	cup flour		

INSTRUCTIONS:

Place all ingredients in a blender. Cover and blend 30 seconds or until combined. Fill 6–8 well greased cups or popover tins half way. Bake in a 400 degree oven for 40 minutes. Remove from cups. Serve with hot butter. For crispy popovers, prick top with a fork to let steam escape before removing from the oven.

Okay, here is the way I do it! I preheat the oven, putting the popover pans or custard cups into the oven for about 10 minutes. Then I put the ingredients in the blender and do pulses until they're well combined. I take the pan out of hot oven, then with a stick of butter, grease the pans well, and fill them. My mixture does about 6 cups. I usually do a double batch. I even make them up ahead of time and then just zap with the blender or take a whisk to them, pour in cups and pop them in the oven!

the mitchell family's famous banana bread

Shared by Tricia Mitchell, Foxboro, Massachusetts

I like to make this with the kids on a Saturday or Sunday. We often make it to share with guests, friends and neighbors. We like to change the recipe sometimes. For instance, one time we added sour cream and found it to be very moist. Another time we added chocolate chips. YUM! And once we added cinnamon sugar on top. Most recently, instead of bananas, we added a cup of canned pumpkin puree, some cinnamon and allspice and made pumpkin bread. Delicious. The kids like to experiment and these are our "secret ingredients".

1¹/₃ cups all purpose flour	1 cup very ripe bananas, mashed, about 2 bananas
³/₄ teaspoon salt	
¹/₂ teaspoon baking soda	¹/₂ cup walnuts or pecans, coarsely chopped, optional
¹/₄ teaspoon baking powder	
5¹/₃ tablespoons unsalted butter, softened	³/₄ cup chocolate chips, optional
²/₃ cup sugar	2 tablespoons sugar
2 large eggs, lightly beaten	1 tablespoon cinnamon
¹/₂ cup sour cream	

INSTRUCTIONS:

Have all ingredients at room temperature. Position oven rack in lower third of oven. Preheat oven to 350 degrees and grease a 6-cup loaf pan. In a bowl, mix first 4 ingredients together thoroughly. In a larger bowl, using a mixer, beat butter and sugar on high speed until light and fluffy, about 2–3 minutes. Beat in flour mixture, a little at a time, until blended and the consistency of brown sugar. Gradually beat in eggs and the sour cream. Next, fold in the mashed bananas, nuts and chocolate chips by hand, until just combined.

Scrape the batter into the pan and spread evenly. Combine sugar and cinnamon and sprinkle mixture on top. Bake until a toothpick inserted in the center comes out clean, about 50–60 minutes. Let cool in the pan on a rack for 5–10 minutes before unmolding to cool completely on the rack.

poppy seed coffeecake

**Shared by Skye Schuyler, Innkeeper, Martin House Inn,
Nantucket, Massachusetts**

CAKE:

1/4	cup poppy seeds	1/4	cup oil
1 1/4	cups cold water	3	eggs
1	box white or yellow cake mix		

GLAZE:

1	cup powdered sugar	1	teaspoon lemon peel, grated
1	tablespoon freshly squeezed lemon juice	1-2	teaspoons water

INSTRUCTIONS:

Soak poppy seeds in cold water for 3 minutes. Preheat oven to 350 degrees. Blend cake mix, oil, eggs and poppy seed liquid in mixing bowl; beat for 4 minutes. Pour into greased bundt pan. Bake for 40-45 minutes.

Cool 10 minutes. Remove from pan and cool completely on wire rack. Mix glaze to make a smooth consistency to drizzle over the cake. Serves 16.

breakfast burrito

Shared by John Reagan, Dot's Diner, Wilmington, Vermont

¹/₂	cup Spanish onion, diced		pinch garlic, granulated
¹/₂	cup mixed peppers, diced		pinch Cajun seasoning
1	cup chicken breast, cooked and diced	4–5	eggs
¹/₄	cup salsa olive oil, for sautéing	2	10-inch wraps
¹/₈	cup jalapeños, diced	¹/₂	cup Monterey Jack cheese, shredded

INSTRUCTIONS:

Sauté onion, peppers, chicken and half of salsa in olive oil. Add all seasonings. Scramble eggs and slightly warm wraps. Combine chicken mixture, eggs and small amount of cheese in wrap, and wrap, and then tuck ends. Drizzle a little salsa and cheese on top and place in oven until cheese is melted. Serves 2.

pantry

sesame granola

bread and butter pickles

maple cinnamon walnuts

harold waterman's bar-be-cue sauce

my favorite salad dressing

herbed pecorino dipping oil

caramelized pecans

cranberry pear apple chutney

cajun aioli

mustard maple vinaigrette

bell pepper relish

cranberry relish

cranberry pear relish

buttermilk dressing

red wine vinaigrette

oven dried tomatoes

sesame granola

Shared by Mountain Village Farm B & B,
Kingfield, Maine

Mountain Village Farm B & B offers a full
organic breakfast menu with several delicious choices.
Farm fresh organic eggs are from my free range hens,
and sausage, bacon and Canadian bacon are from my all
natural fed pastured pigs. Sesame granola is a favorite with
hikers and skiers for its wholesome and satisfying quality.
Many guests use it for trail mix.

2 cups uncooked rolled oats	1/2 cup coconut flakes, optional
2 cups wheat flakes	1/2 cup vegetable oil
1 cup sunflower seeds	1/2 cup honey
1 cup raisins	1 teaspoon vanilla extract
3/4 cup sesame seeds	
1/2 cup walnuts, chopped	

INSTRUCTIONS:

Preheat oven to 350 degrees. Combine all dry ingredients. Heat oil, honey and vanilla in saucepan to a boil. Add the dry ingredients and mix well.

Place on a 13 x 9 baking pan and bake 15–20 minutes until golden brown. Allow to cool before removing.

bread and butter pickles

Shared by Marge Williams, Guilford, Connecticut

*This is a recipe that my family has been using for years.
I use fresh cucumbers out of my garden every summer
and can jars and jars of these wonderful pickles.
This recipe is one adapted from Woman's Home
Companion Cookbook, 1942.*

6	quarts medium size cucumbers, thinly sliced	2	cups water
6	white medium size onions, thinly sliced	1	quart vinegar
		4	cups sugar
3/4	cup salt	2	tablespoons celery seed
		2	tablespoons mustard seed

INSTRUCTIONS:

Wash cucumbers thoroughly before slicing. Arrange sliced cucumbers and onions in layers in an earthenware crock or bowl. Sprinkle each layer with salt. Cover and let stand 3 hours. Drain off the juice that has accumulated.

Combine water, vinegar, sugar, celery seed and mustard seed. Bring to a boil, stirring until sugar is dissolved; boil for 3 minutes. Add cucumber mixture and bring once more to the boiling point but do not boil.

Pack immediately into hot sterilized jars. Seal at once. Makes about 8 pints.

maple cinnamon walnuts

Shared by Kate Walston, Guilford, Connecticut

Using pure maple syrup is a must when making these nuts. I have always been lucky to use maple syrup made by my family farm right here in Guilford, Connecticut. This technique of candying the nuts was taught to me when I was a student at the Natural Gourmet Cookery School in New York City.

1	teaspoon cinnamon	$^{2}/_{3}$	cup pure maple syrup
$^{1}/_{2}$	teaspoon salt	4	cups whole walnuts
2	teaspoons vanilla		

INSTRUCTIONS:

Preheat oven to 350 degrees. Line a sheet tray (or baking pan with sidewalls) with parchment paper. Whisk together first 4 ingredients; add walnuts and toss to coat. Pour nut mixture onto prepared pan and set timer for 30 minutes. Begin baking. Every 10 minutes pull out the tray and with a spoon toss and recoat nuts. Continue this process until syrup is no longer runny; finished nuts will be crusty. Allow to cool, then break apart clustered nuts and serve or store airtight.

harold waterman's bar-be-cue sauce

Shared by Suzie Birks, Madison, Connecticut

*My sister put together a Hodge family cookbook in 1992.
My favorite is my cousin Harold Waterman's sauce,
a recipe he brought back from Texas probably in the 50s.
It is the best ever on chicken for a large crowd. I marinate the
chicken in half the sauce and baste with the rest. With all the
butter, it will burn so you have to be careful while grilling it.*

1	pound butter	3	teaspoons Tabasco sauce
6	lemons, juiced	1/2	jar horseradish
1/3	cup ketchup		

INSTRUCTIONS:

Combine all ingredients and use half for marinating and half for grilling.

my favorite salad dressing

Shared by Mary Malchodi Dodd, Stamford, Connecticut

1	cup extra virgin olive oil	1	tablespoon Dijon mustard
1/4	cup balsamic vinegar		salt, to taste
1	teaspoon honey		pepper, to taste

INSTRUCTIONS:

Mix all ingredients in a bowl and serve over salad or pasta.

herbed pecorino dipping oil

Shared by a local in Hartland, Vermont

1 teaspoon dried oregano	pinch salt
1 teaspoon dried basil	4 teaspoons pecorino cheese
1/2 cup extra virgin olive oil freshly ground black pepper, to taste	crusty baguettes or ciabatta for dipping

INSTRUCTIONS:

Combine seasoning and olive oil in bowl. Then pour half the amount in shallow plate. Top with half of the pecorino cheese. Dip pieces of crusty bread into oil. Makes 2 plates.

caramelized pecans

Shared by Bill Wooton, Corner Cafe, Newport, Rhode Island

3 tablespoons sugar	1/4 cup pecans
1/2 teaspoon water	2 pinches cinnamon

INSTRUCTIONS:

In small saucepan, bring sugar and water to boil; add pecans and cinnamon. Mix until pecans are coated. Bake in oven at 350 degrees for 5–10 minutes or until sugar crystallizes.

cranberry pear apple chutney

**Shared by Lisa Battilana, Executive Chef,
Woodstock Farmers' Market, Woodstock, Vermont**

This is great with Thanksgiving dinner.

3	cups cranberries	1	tablespoon lemon zest
1	cup sugar	1	tablespoon lemon juice
3	firm pears	1/4	cup dried dates, pitted
1	firm apple, Granny Smith, Northern Spy or other	1/4	cup golden raisins
		1/2	cup orange juice

INSTRUCTIONS:

Combine cranberries and sugar. Cook over medium-low heat until berries begin to pop open, about 8 minutes. Peel, core and cut pears and apple into 1/2 inch diced pieces. Place in bowl and toss with lemon zest and juice.

Coarsely chop dates and combine with raisins and orange juice. When the cranberries have begun to pop, add the orange juice, raisin and date mixture to the pot with the cranberries. Raise heat to medium, stirring frequently. When mixture bubbles, add pears and apple. Cook, stirring until mixture thickens, pears turn red and are cooked through.

Pour finished chutney into a glass bowl or jar, cool and cover. Refrigerate. This will keep for 3 weeks.

cajun aioli

Shared by Coffee's Country Market, Old Lyme, Connecticut

1	cup mayonnaise		zest of 1 lime
5	scallions, cleaned and finely chopped		juice of 1 lime
		2–3	tablespoons Cajun spice mix

INSTRUCTIONS:

Combine all ingredients and mix well.

mustard maple vinaigrette

Shared by Bluebird Restaurant and Ruth, Machias, Maine

3	tablespoons balsamic vinegar	½	cup olive oil
1	tablespoon maple syrup		salt, to taste
1	teaspoon Dijon mustard		pepper, to taste

INSTRUCTIONS:

Whisk together first 3 ingredients, then the oil, salt and pepper.

bell pepper relish

Shared by Loretta Tallevast, Lake City, South Carolina

1	dozen green peppers	2	pints vinegar
1	dozen red peppers	4	tablespoons salt
1	dozen onions	2	cups sugar

INSTRUCTIONS:

Grind peppers and onions and pour off juice. Pour boiling water over cut peppers and onions and let stand for 10 minutes. Drain well. Mix vinegar, salt and sugar. Add to peppers and onions and bring to boiling point. Cook for 10 minutes.

Put in jars and seal. Makes 4 quarts.

cranberry relish

Shared by Jo Ellen Odom, Lake City, South Carolina

1	pound fresh cranberries	2	apples, pared and cored
2	oranges, peeled and sliced	2	cups sugar

INSTRUCTIONS:

Grind first 3 ingredients in food processor using fine blade. Add sugar and mix well. Chill. Keep several days in refrigerator.

cranberry pear relish

Shared by Ellen Maguire, Madison, Connecticut

This is an old recipe that was cut out of a magazine years ago and has become one of my favorite relishes to serve with Thanksgiving dinner. It is also delicious with beef tenderloin during the holiday season.

1 1/2 cups sugar
1/2 cup water
1 12-ounce package fresh cranberries

2–3 medium pears, cored and cubed
1/2 teaspoon nutmeg
1/2 teaspoon allspice
1 4-inch stick cinnamon

INSTRUCTIONS:

In a 2-quart saucepan, bring sugar and water to boiling, stirring to dissolve sugar. Boil rapidly, uncovered, for 5 minutes. Add remaining ingredients and return to boiling. Cook for 3–4 minutes, until cranberry skins pop, stirring occasionally. Remove from heat. Cover and chill. This will keep for up to 1 week. Enjoy.

buttermilk dressing

Shared by Lisa Battilana, Executive Chef,
Woodstock Farmers' Market, Woodstock, Vermont

1 1/2 cups mayonnaise	salt, to taste
3/4 cup buttermilk	pepper, to taste
1 1/2 tablespoons garlic, finely minced	1 teaspoon paprika
	2 teaspoons Tabasco sauce

INSTRUCTIONS:

Combine and whisk together all dressing ingredients. Taste carefully for salt and Tabasco; adjust as needed. Use on your favorite salad.

red wine vinaigrette

Shared by Loretta Tallevast, Lake City, South Carolina

3/4 cup oil	1/4 teaspoon pepper
1/2 cup red wine vinegar	2 cloves garlic, chopped
1/2 teaspoon salt	

INSTRUCTIONS:

Whisk together ingredients.

oven dried tomatoes

Shared by Mary Malchodi Dodd, Stamford, Connecticut

I love to play around with existing recipes. Here is my favorite. I reworked an old recipe and changed the herbs and garlic. I use this in panini sandwiches or as part of an omelette.

24	Roma plum tomatoes, sliced in half	6	tablespoons extra virgin olive oil, extra for storage
	sea salt, to taste	2	tablespoons Herbes de Provence
	freshly ground pepper, to taste	3–5	cloves garlic, minced

INSTRUCTIONS:

Preheat the oven to 250 degrees. Line the baking sheet with a silpat or parchment paper for easy cleanup. Arrange tomato halves cut side up and close together on a baking sheet. Season with salt and pepper to taste. In a small bowl, combine the olive oil with herbs and garlic. Spoon a little bit on each tomato. Bake until the tomatoes are soft and shriveled but still retain some moisture, which takes about 5–8 hours. Timing depends on how large, meaty and juicy the tomatoes are. Let cool completely and then store in a container with a layer of olive oil over the top of each tomato. Cover tightly and refrigerate. Keeps for 1 week in the refrigerator.

soups & salads

lyn's strawberry chicken salad

cornbread salad

avocado summer salad

downeast summer salad

autumn harvest soup

broccoli salad

italian summer salad

curried chicken salad

beer cheese soup

strawberry salad

warm toasted bijou salad

mixed greens with seared scallops

steamer clam chowder

strawberry soup

creamy spinach bisque

soups & salads

beef barley soup with short ribs

grilled peaches

chicken and corn chili

thai eggplant and green bean salad

country tomato soup

john's carrot soup

andrea's curried apple soup

orzo with smoked turkey
and bacon buttermilk dressing

july 4th potato salad

corn chowder

rutabaga bisque

butternut squash soup

english spring pea and mint soup

lyn's strawberry chicken salad

Shared by Bill Wooton, Corner Cafe, Newport, Rhode Island

5	large fresh strawberries	2	ounces balsamic vinaigrette
¹/₂	cup balsamic vinegar		
1	6-ounce chicken breast	¹/₄	cup caramelized pecans *(see recipe page 101)*
4–5	cups mesclun salad mix		
1	ounce Parmesan cheese, grated	2	ounces goat cheese, crumbled

INSTRUCTIONS:

One day before preparing: Chop 4 of the strawberries and marinate in ¹/₂ cup vinegar. Refrigerate overnight.

Grill chicken breast and slice lengthwise. In a medium mixing bowl, toss greens, Parmesan cheese and balsamic vinaigrette. Place in serving bowl. Top with pecans, strawberries and goat cheese. Lay sliced chicken breast over top. Place reserved strawberry off center for garnish. Serve with side of balsamic vinaigrette.

cornbread salad

Shared by Brenda Martin, Charleston, South Carolina

1	box Jiffy cornbread mix	1	pound bacon, fried and crumbled
1	medium green bell pepper, chopped	1½	cups mayonnaise
1	medium onion, chopped	1	tablespoon sugar
3–5	pounds tomatoes, chopped	½	cup salad cube pickles

INSTRUCTIONS:

Prepare cornbread as directed on package. Crumble half of baked cornbread in bottom of a 9 x 13 dish. Layer bell pepper, onion, tomatoes and crumbled bacon in order listed, saving enough bacon for the top. Combine mayonnaise, sugar and pickles. Spread on top of salad. Crumble remaining cornbread on top and then sprinkle with remaining bacon. Serves 6–8.

avocado summer salad

Shared by Sarah Galluzzo, Fairfield, Connecticut

I was roasting a clove of garlic for my red sauce and grabbing stuff from the fridge and garden and I whipped up this new, complex in texture and flavor salad that eats like a meal. Pack in your lunch and you won't be hungry all day. Can you imagine this as a summer sandwich? I thought I had better write it down before I forgot what I did.

DRESSING:

1   overripe avocado, halved
1–2 drops balsamic vinegar
    handful of chickpeas

    splash orange muscat
    champagne vinegar
2   small cloves garlic, roasted
1   lime, juiced

SALAD:

1   can chickpeas, drained
1   large tomato, chopped
½ red onion, finely chopped

1   garden cucumber,
    chopped in chunks
    salt, to taste
    pepper, to taste

INSTRUCTIONS:

Whip up all the dressing ingredients with an immersion blender and set aside. Combine all the ingredients for the salad in a bowl and top with the lovely green dressing. Coat well. Serve and smile, Baby!

downeast summer salad
with mustard maple vinaigrette

Shared by Bluebird Restaurant and Ruth, Machias, Maine

DRESSING:

3 tablespoons balsamic vinegar	½ cup olive oil
1 tablespoon maple syrup	salt, to taste
1 teaspoon Dijon mustard	pepper, to taste

SALAD:

4-6 cups seasonal greens	²/₃ cup dried cranberries
20 sugar snap peas	²/₃ cup walnuts, toasted
²/₃ cup fresh blueberries (I use Maine wild blueberries)	²/₃ cup local goat cheese, crumbled

INSTRUCTIONS:

For the dressing, whisk together first 3 ingredients, then the oil, salt and pepper.

Spread greens on platter or individual plates, top with remaining 5 ingredients. Drizzle with vinaigrette and serve. Serves 4–5.

autumn harvest soup

Shared by Frankie Morrow, Winhall, Vermont

This recipe is a favorite for foliage season and I have been making huge amounts at the Pumpkin Festival in Townsend, Vermont, every October since 2001. It is now something that a lot of people request.

2–3 large Spanish onions, chopped

2–3 cloves garlic, chopped

1 butternut squash, peeled and roughly diced

4 potatoes, chopped

4–5 big carrots, chopped

3 sweet potatoes, chopped

3–4 cups pumpkin flesh, or 28 ounce can pumpkin puree

3 apples, any kind, peeled and diced

chicken or vegetarian stock, enough to cover all vegetables

milk or cream, enough to make soup creamy after blending

coriander, to taste

nutmeg, to taste

allspice, to taste

ginger, to taste

cloves, to taste

salt, to taste

pepper, to taste

fresh cilantro

fresh mountain mint

INSTRUCTIONS:

Sauté onions, then garlic. Quickly add all veggies and stock. Bring back to boil and simmer until veggies are tender. Blend or puree and add enough milk to make mixture creamy. Spice with ground coriander, nutmeg, allspice, ginger and cloves. Salt and pepper to taste, then jazz it up with fresh cilantro or mountain mint.

broccoli salad

Shared by Loretta Tallevast, Lake City, South Carolina

2 crowns uncooked broccoli, cut into bite size pieces	1/2 onion, finely chopped
	2 cups sharp cheddar cheese, grated
1/2 pound crispy bacon, crumbled	1/2 cup raisins
	1 ounce almonds, sliced

INSTRUCTIONS:

Toss all ingredients together.

DRESSING:

1 cup mayonnaise	1 tablespoon lemon juice
1/2 cup sugar	1 teaspoon poppy seeds
2 tablespoons apple cider vinegar	

INSTRUCTIONS:

Combine all ingredients and pour dressing over salad. Refrigerate for at least 3 hours before serving. Keeps up to 1 week in the refrigerator. Serves 4–6.

italian summer salad

Shared by Sardella's Restaurant, Newport, Rhode Island
Easy and delicious!

1	large head iceberg lettuce, chopped into 1-inch strips	1/2	cup extra virgin olive oil
1	large cucumber, cut into chunks	1/8	cup red wine vinegar
3	large ripe tomatoes, cut into wedges	3	cloves garlic, diced
		1/4	teaspoon fresh oregano, chopped

INSTRUCTIONS:

Put the chopped lettuce, cucumber and tomatoes in a large salad bowl and toss. In a small carafe, add the oil, vinegar, garlic and oregano and stir briskly. Add the dressing to the bowl and toss. Serve on chilled salad plates. Serves 2.

curried chicken salad

Shared by Simon's Marketplace, Chester, Connecticut

4   large chicken breasts, baked and diced in large pieces

1   cup raisins

¹⁄₂ cup orange juice

1   Granny Smith apple, diced with skin

³⁄₄ cup walnuts, chopped

2   stalks celery, chopped

1   tablespoon curry powder

¹⁄₂ teaspoon salt

¹⁄₂ cup mayonnaise

INSTRUCTIONS:

Poach or bake chicken and cool. Add raisins and orange juice to saucepan and bring to a boil. Remove from heat and put in refrigerator to cool. When cooled, add all ingredients except mayonnaise and toss gently until curry has evenly coated everything. Add mayonnaise and toss again.

beer cheese soup

*Shared by Kathleen Campbell, Cornucopia Wine and Cheese
Market, Stratham, New Hampshire*

1	stick salted butter	4–5	cans low salt chicken broth
2	carrots, finely chopped		
2	celery sticks, finely chopped	8	ounces Coastal Cheddar* from England, grated
1	small onion, finely chopped	1	bottle flat beer, can use Harp-Irish beer
2–4	tablespoons cornstarch		lobster, shrimp, scallops, optional

INSTRUCTIONS:

Melt ½ stick butter in pot. Sauté vegetables until clear but not brown.
Add rest of butter. Add cornstarch slowly and stir. Pour in chicken broth
slowly while stirring. Slowly add cheese, continuing to stir while the
cheese melts. Then slowly add beer. Stir until smooth and creamy.
Lobster, shrimp or scallops may be added. Serve in a soup bowl with
warm, crusty Tuscan ciabatta. Serves 4. *See reference page 307

mixed greens with seared scallops

Shared by Lorraine King, Hampton, New Hampshire

SALAD:

	assortment of mixed greens		salt, to taste
8	large sea scallops		pepper, to taste
2	tablespoons olive oil	2	tablespoons butter

VINAIGRETTE:

1/2	cup Maine wild blueberries		salt, to taste
1	shallot, finely chopped		pepper, to taste
1/4	cup olive oil	2	tablespoons Parmesan cheese, shredded
1	lemon, zest and juice		

INSTRUCTIONS:

Divide mixed greens on 4 plates. Season scallops with salt and pepper. Heat olive oil and butter in a sauté pan and fry the scallops quickly on high heat, 1–2 minutes on each side. Remove from heat. Top the greens with scallops.

In the same sauté pan, mix blueberries, shallots, oil, lemon juice and zest. Bring mixture to a boil, crushing some of the blueberries. Season with salt and pepper and add more lemon juice if needed. Pour vinaigrette over scallops and top with Parmesan cheese. Serves 4.

steamer clam chowder

Shared by Black Point Inn, Prouts Neck, Scarborough, Maine

This recipe uses steamer clams freshly dug on Sand Dollar Beach! It is best to leave the clams overnight in seawater with 1/8 cup of cornmeal over the water. This will help them to filter out any sand in their bellies.

5 pounds fresh steamer clams or 1 pound shucked clams	1 medium Turkish bay leaf
	¼ cup flour
1 cup water	2 large russet potatoes, peeled and cubed
⅓ pound smoked bacon, diced	¼ cup dry sherry
1 stick butter	1½ cups heavy cream
2 ribs celery, diced	2½ cups milk
1 medium onion, diced	salt, to taste
2 teaspoons fresh thyme	pepper, to taste

INSTRUCTIONS:

Begin by steaming clams in deep stock pot until they open. Add 1 cup water so they do not dry out. Strain cooking broth to add to chowder later. Pull the clams out and pull off the siphons to the arrowhead shaped meat. Discard all but this meat and the soft belly. In 2-quart, heavy-bottomed nonreactive stock pot, gently brown diced bacon. Remove cooked bacon, leaving the fat.

Add butter, celery, onion, thyme and bay leaf. Gently cook until onion and celery are soft, about 10 minutes. Add flour and mix in well to make roux. Cook 3–5 minutes on low heat. Add potatoes, clam meat, broth and sherry. Mix and add heavy cream and simmer until potatoes are cooked through. Finally, add the milk, being careful not to let chowder boil. Season to taste with salt and pepper. Garnish with chopped bacon. Serves 4.

strawberry soup

*Shared by Peter Ross, Executive Chef, Middlebury Inn,
Middlebury, Vermont*

*This is famous at our inn, always requested by our locals
and guests.*

1	pint fresh strawberries	¼	cup sugar, more if you
1	cup sour cream		have a sweet tooth!
2	cups half and half		pinch salt
3	tablespoons brandy		mint, for garnish

INSTRUCTIONS:

Place all the ingredients in a blender or use a stick blender and puree
until smooth. Keep chilled in the refrigerator until ready to serve. Garnish
with fresh strawberries and sprig of mint.

creamy spinach bisque
with bacon and fried shallots

Shared by Peter Sullivan, The Stage Neck Inn, York, Maine

2	pieces raw bacon	6	cups baby spinach
1	tablespoon roasted garlic	1/2	cup parsley, chopped
1	shallot, chopped	1	shallot for frying
2	cups heavy cream		flour, for tossing with shallot rings
1	tablespoon lemon zest		
1	tablespoon salt		Old Bay seasoning, to taste
1/2	tablespoon black pepper		

INSTRUCTIONS:

On medium heat, cook chopped bacon with garlic. Add shallot; sweat lightly. Add cream, lemon zest, and salt and pepper. When cream scalds, add spinach and parsley, then turn off the heat. Use a hand blender or pour into a blender and puree.

Slice second shallot into rings. Toss with flour and Old Bay seasoning. Deep fry and put on top of the bisque before serving.

beef barley soup with short ribs

Shared by Robin Walston, Stratham, New Hampshire

A neighbor made this soup for Ray and me after we brought Mia home from the hospital. I have been making it ever since. It is a great fall/winter soup and is perfect as a meal when served with some really great crusty bread.

2½–3	pounds beef short ribs	½	teaspoon Worcestershire sauce
2	tablespoons oil	2	cups carrots, sliced
8	cups water	1	cup celery, sliced
2	15-ounce cans diced tomatoes, undrained	½	cup green pepper, chopped
1	large onion, chopped	⅔	cup quick cook barley
2	tablespoons instant bouillon cubes	4	cups parsley, chopped
1½	teaspoons salt		salt, to taste
1	teaspoon dried basil, crushed		pepper, to taste
			parmesan cheese, to taste

INSTRUCTIONS:

In a large kettle or Dutch oven, brown short ribs in hot oil over low heat; drain well. Stir in water, tomatoes, onion, bouillon cubes, salt, basil and Worcestershire sauce. Cover and simmer for 1½ hours. Stir in carrots, celery, green pepper, barley, and parsley. Cover and simmer for 45 minutes. Remove ribs; when cool enough to handle, cut off any meat and coarsely chop. Discard bones. Skim fat from soup. Return meat to soup and heat through. Season to taste with salt and pepper. Serve with fresh Parmesan cheese and crusty bread. Serves 8–10.

grilled peaches
with goat cheese, honey and cinnamon

Shared by Formaggio Kitchen, Cambridge, Massachusetts

Simple and delicious.

4	peaches	1/4	cup chestnut honey
1/8	cup sugar	1	tablespoon Vietnamese
1	cup unsalted goat cheese		cinnamon

INSTRUCTIONS:

Preheat grill to medium-high heat. Meanwhile, cut the peaches in half and discard the pits. Sprinkle each half with a thin layer of sugar and place the peaches on the grill, cut side down. Grill the peaches for 10–15 minutes or until the sugar caramelizes and they are tender; timing will depend on the ripeness of the peaches.

Remove the peaches from the grill and fill each center with the goat cheese. Drizzle with chestnut honey, sprinkle with cinnamon and serve. This is a nice side to chicken or pork. You can also add a scoop of ice cream; it makes a wonderful dessert.

chicken and corn chili

Shared by Diane Gardner, Madison, Connecticut
**This is something I made one day while looking
for a "lighter" chili. It's quick and easy.**

1	large onion, chopped		salt, to taste
5	cloves garlic, chopped		pepper, to taste
2	pounds ground chicken or turkey	2	cans black beans, drained
4	large cans whole plum tomatoes	2	cans white beans, drained
1½	pounds spicy chicken sausage	2	cans red beans, drained
2	packs chili seasoning, 1 regular, 1 spicy hot	6	ears corn, cut off cob, or 1 small bag frozen corn kernels
2	big shakes crushed red pepper		sour cream, to taste
			sharp cheddar cheese, grated
			onions, chopped

INSTRUCTIONS:

Sauté onion and garlic in large pot. As these start to brown, add ground chicken and cook well. Drain off all fat, add plum tomatoes and let simmer. Meanwhile bake the chicken sausage at 350 degrees until done, then slice in bite size pieces and toss in simmering tomato sauce. Add chili seasoning and red pepper flakes, salt and pepper to taste and let simmer for about 45 minutes.

Add all drained beans and stir well. Add corn and let come to a slow boil. Turn off and let sit a little while. Serve with sour cream, grated sharp cheddar and chopped onions.

thai eggplant and green bean salad

Shared by Lisa Battilana, Executive Chef,
Woodstock Farmers' Market, Woodstock, Vermont

The classic combination of sweet, salty and sour tastes are captured in this unique salad, utilizing vegetables which are all at their peak during mid to late summer in New England.

VEGETABLES:

3 **medium size eggplants, cut into 1-inch chunks**	1 **basket cherry tomatoes, halved**
¼ **cup vegetable oil**	½ **cup toasted peanuts, coarsely chopped**
2 **pounds green beans, stemmed**	

DRESSING:

¼ **cup fresh lime juice**	1½ **teaspoons garlic, minced**
½ **cup sugar**	1 **bunch cilantro, chopped**
½ **cup fish sauce**	3 **teaspoons vegetable oil**

INSTRUCTIONS:

Toss eggplant with vegetable oil. Spread on a sheet pan and roast in a 350 degree oven approximately 20 minutes or until cooked through and lightly browned. Cool completely.

Blanch the green beans in 3 quarts of salted boiling water for 3 minutes. Drain beans and place in ice water to stop further cooking.

In a medium size bowl, combine lime juice and sugar. Stir to dissolve the sugar. Add fish sauce and garlic. Set aside a small amount of cilantro to garnish salad, then add the remainder and the vegetable oil to the dressing. Whisk to combine.

Toss together vegetables and dressing. Place salad on a low sided platter or in a shallow bowl and top with reserved cilantro, tomatoes and peanuts.

country tomato soup

Shared by The Governor's House in Hyde Park, Vermont
This is served as a first course,
usually for a wedding dinner. Enjoy.

1	yellow onion, chopped	1	cup heavy cream or plain yogurt
2	cloves garlic, chopped		
3	tablespoons olive oil	1/2	teaspoon salt
3	cups chicken or vegetable stock	1/4	teaspoon coarsely ground pepper
20	ounces tomatoes	1 1/2	teaspoons brown sugar

INSTRUCTIONS:

Sauté onion and garlic in oil for 5 minutes. Add stock and tomatoes.
Bring to a boil and simmer for 15 minutes. Remove from heat and cool
slightly. Puree tomatoes if too chunky, or puree just some. Return to pot
and add remaining ingredients while warming, but do not boil. Serves 8.

john's carrot soup

Shared by John Marsala, Branford, Connecticut

2	pounds carrots, cleaned and chopped	3	tablespoons butter
4	cups chicken stock	1	cup milk
1½	teaspoons salt	1	cup yogurt
½	teaspoon cinnamon	½	cup heavy cream
1	onion, chopped	¾	cup sour cream
1–2	small cloves garlic, crushed		fresh ginger root, grated
			sour cream, to taste

INSTRUCTIONS:

Bring the first 4 ingredients to a boil and simmer for 10 minutes. Sauté together the onion and garlic in butter. Puree these ingredients together until well blended. Return to the pot and whisk in the milk, yogurt, heavy cream and sour cream and heat very slowly. Garnish with ginger root and sour cream. Serve and enjoy.

andrea's curried apple soup

Shared by Andrea Scott, Champlain Orchards, Shoreham, Vermont

2	medium onions, peeled and chopped	¹/₄	teaspoon cloves
4	tablespoons butter	¹/₄	teaspoon cinnamon
1	teaspoon fresh ginger, grated	¹/₄	teaspoon cayenne
1	teaspoon dry mustard	6	tart apples*, chopped
1	teaspoon turmeric	1¹/₂	quarts chicken stock
1	teaspoon ground cumin	1	lemon, juiced
1	teaspoon ground coriander		salt, to taste
			pepper, to taste
			sour cream, to taste

INSTRUCTIONS:

Sauté onions in butter. Add the next 8 spices. Cook slightly to "toast". Add apples and chicken stock, and simmer until apples are soft. Reserve 1 cup of apple pieces to add later to soup if desired. Puree soup in food processor. Add lemon juice and season to taste. Serve with sour cream. Serves 6.

*See reference page 307

orzo
with smoked turkey and bacon buttermilk dressing

Shared by Lisa Battilana, Executive Chef,
Woodstock Farmers' Market, Woodstock, Vermont

Of the hundreds of salads made at Woodstock Farmers'
Market, this is a favorite with our customers.

4	cups dry orzo	6	strips bacon
1/2	pound smoked turkey, cut in 1/2 inch slices and cubed	1	bunch scallions, thinly sliced
		1	cup frozen peas, thawed

INSTRUCTIONS:

Bring to a boil 1 gallon of salted water. Add orzo and cook according to package directions. Drain cooked orzo in a colander and refresh with cold water to halt cooking. Spread orzo on a sheet pan and cool completely. While the pasta is cooking, fry the bacon slices until crisp. Cool and chop coarsely.

When the above ingredients are cool, toss together with turkey, scallions and peas in a large bowl. Prepare dressing.

BUTTERMILK DRESSING:

1 1/2	cups mayonnaise		salt, to taste
3/4	cup buttermilk		pepper, to taste
1 1/2	tablespoons garlic, finely minced	1	teaspoon paprika
		2	teaspoons Tabasco sauce

INSTRUCTIONS:

Combine and whisk together all dressing ingredients. Taste carefully for salt and Tabasco; adjust as needed.

Mix half of the dressing with orzo. Add more to taste and desired consistency.

july 4th potato salad

Shared by Community of Christ Church, Jonesport, Maine

1 **pound each of red, white and blue new potatoes, scrubbed and left unpeeled**	**ground pepper, to taste** **salt, to taste**
¹⁄₂ **pound smoked bacon, sliced**	4 **stalks celery, minced**
1 **large red onion, minced**	3 **tablespoons fresh parsley, minced**
¹⁄₂ **cup cider vinegar**	3 **tablespoons fresh tarragon, minced**
¹⁄₂ **cup dry white wine**	**hard boiled eggs, large chunks, optional**
4 **tablespoons olive oil**	

INSTRUCTIONS:

Place all the potatoes together in a pot and bring to a boil, then simmer until fork tender, about 25–30 minutes. Drain well. While the potatoes are cooking, brown the bacon until crisp; remove and drain on paper towels. Add the onions to the bacon fat in the pan and sauté until softened, about 5 minutes. Swirl in the vinegar, wine and olive oil. Season the mixture with salt and pepper and keep warm over low heat.

Cut the hot potatoes into coarse chunks and toss with the celery in a large mixing bowl. Pour the warm bacon dressing over the potatoes, stirring to coat thoroughly. Mix in the parsley and tarragon. Crumble the bacon and eggs into the salad. Serve warm or at room temperature.

corn chowder

Shared by Denise Butcher, Ship's Knees Inn,
East Orleans, Massachusetts

Denise and Peter Butcher met at Ship's Knees Inn in the summer of 1972. Today they own the inn and welcome every guest as if you are a part of their family. This is truly a special and unique inn nestled in the beautiful Cape!

2	cups boiling water	1	17-ounce creamed corn
2	cups potatoes, diced	1	17-ounce can corn
1/2	cup carrots, diced	1/4	cup butter
1/2	cup celery, diced	1/4	cup flour
1/4	cup onion, chopped	2	cups milk or half and half
1 1/2	teaspoons salt		salt, to taste
1/4	teaspoon pepper		bacon, fried and
1/4	teaspoon thyme		chopped, to taste
1	cup sharp cheddar		parsley, chopped, to taste
	cheese, shredded		basil, chopped, to taste

INSTRUCTIONS:

Boil in water, potatoes, carrots, celery, onion, salt, pepper and thyme for 15–20 minutes. Add cheese and both cans of corn. Set aside. Make a white sauce in another pan by combining butter, flour and milk; stir until thick. Combine with the corn mixture and simmer on medium-low until thoroughly cooked. To serve, adjust seasoning with salt as needed and top with bacon, parsley and basil.

rutabaga bisque
maple style

Shared by Frankie Morrow, Winhall, Vermont

½	cup butter	1	cup heavy cream
1	cup leeks, chopped	3–4	tablespoons dark maple syrup
2–3	green onions, chopped		salt, to taste
5	cups rutabaga, cubed		pepper, to taste
2	cups chicken or vegetable stock		chives, for garnish

INSTRUCTIONS:

In a large soup pot, melt butter. Cook leeks and onions until translucent. Add rutabaga and sauté for 3–4 minutes. Add stock and bring to a boil, then simmer for 30–40 minutes or until tender. Blend or puree. Add cream and maple syrup, warm a bit and season to taste with salt and pepper. Garnish with chopped chives before serving.

butternut squash soup

Shared by Betsy Rudden, Farmington, Connecticut

This started as a basic soup and has evolved into a multilayered concoction using some of my favorite ingredients. I make this all winter long and deliver to my neighbors, many of whom are elderly and don't cook much anymore. Of all the soups I make, they always ask for this one again and again. It is good on the first day and freezes well, too.

3 pounds butternut squash, peeled, seeded and cut into 2-inch chunks

1 pound parsnips, peeled and cut into rough chunks

1 celery root, peeled and cut into rough chunks

1 large white onion, peeled and rough cut
   salt, to taste
   pepper, to taste

   olive oil, for tossing
   balsamic vinegar, for tossing

1 small can diced tomatoes with garlic

2 cups beef or veal stock

3 cups good chicken stock

1 tablespoon cumin

1 cup half and half
   sour cream, for garnish

INSTRUCTIONS:

Preheat oven to 400 degrees to roast the vegetables. Season the veggies with salt and pepper. Toss squash, parsnips, celery root and onion in a bowl with enough olive oil and balsamic to lightly coat. Place on 2 cookie sheets and place in oven. Turn over veggies every 15 minutes for even caramelizing and switch baking sheets so each has a chance to be on the bottom rack. Roast until a fork is easily inserted. Watch closely because these can easily burn.

Transfer veggies to a large pot; add the tomatoes, stock and cumin. Cook so flavors marry for about 30 minutes. Blend using a stick blender or in small batches in a countertop blender. After all ingredients are combined and the mixture is smooth, taste and season with more salt, pepper and cumin as needed. Right before serving, stir in half and half. Serve garnished with a small dollop of sour cream and enjoy.

english spring pea and mint soup
with crème fraiche and candied lemon crostini

Shared by Matthew Jennings, La Laiterie at Farmstead,
Providence, Rhode Island

SOUP:

2   shallots, finely chopped

1 1/2 cups fresh English peas, shelled

1 1/2 tablespoons fresh thyme, lemon thyme if you can find it

5   tablespoons light cream
kosher salt, to taste

cracked black pepper, to taste

1 1/2 tablespoons fresh mint leaves, finely shredded, plus a few whole leaves for garnish

2/3 cup crème fraiche

INSTRUCTIONS:

Bring 3/4 cup of water to a boil in a deep saucepan and then add the shallots, peas, thyme and light cream. Simmer gently for 8–10 minutes or until the peas are completely tender and season this mixture to taste with kosher salt and black pepper.

Next, puree the soup in batches in the food processor or with a hand held blender and then push through a fine mesh sieve for a smoother, more velvety finish if desired.

If serving warm (this soup is great cold, too, in the summer), pour back into clean saucepan, add the shredded mint, reseason if necessary and gently reheat. Otherwise, just stir in the mint and then chill for at least 2–3 hours. To serve, ladle into bowls and swirl crème fraiche into the soup with a spoon. Garnish with mint leaves and crostini, and sprinkle with cracked black pepper. Serves 4.

CROSTINI:

- 1 loaf rustic style French or Italian bread
- ³/₄ cup olive oil
- 1 tablespoon cider vinegar
- 3 tablespoons candied lemon rind, chopped
- 3 large cloves garlic, peeled and thinly sliced
- 2 tablespoons fresh basil, shredded
- 2 tablespoons fresh parsley, chopped

  kosher salt, to taste

  cracked black pepper, to taste

INSTRUCTIONS:

Preheat oven to 350 degrees. Combine all ingredients (except bread). Brush mixture on both sides of bread slices. Toast on baking sheet for 10–15 minutes or until nicely toasted and crisp. If preparing in advance, cool and store in airtight container for up to 1 day.

everyday greens & sides

sweet potato casserole

aunt rose's polenta

elda's stuffing recipe

braised fennel bulbs

risott

asian slaw

garlic green beans

rutabaga with apple cider

praline squash puree

cranberry risotto

mothers home baked beans

bleu cheese gratin

poutines

baked sweet potato fries

pesto mashed potatoes

sweet potato casserole

Given to Marie Walston from Nina, Jonesport, Maine

CASSEROLE:

2 1/2	pounds sweet potatoes	1/2	cup milk
4	tablespoons unsalted butter	2	large eggs
			salt, to taste
1/2	cup granulated sugar	1/2	teaspoon pure vanilla

PECAN TOPPING:

3/4	cup pecans	3	tablespoons flour
1/2	cup light brown sugar, packed	4	tablespoons unsalted butter, cold

INSTRUCTIONS:

Preheat oven to 350 degrees. Butter a 9 x 13 baking dish. Cut potatoes into 2–3 inch chunks and boil in salted water until tender, about 20 minutes. Mash and beat in butter, sugar, milk, eggs, salt and vanilla. Spread into prepared dish.

In a processor pulse pecans until medium fine, pour into bowl and add brown sugar and flour. Add butter and mix with fingers to make a crumb that resembles coarse meal. Sprinkle over sweet potatoes.

Bake 30–40 minutes until topping is golden. Serves 8–10.

aunt rose's polenta

**Shared by Jessica Granatiero, The Savory Grape,
East Greenwich, Rhode Island**

*Other than "Aunt Rose's Polenta", I don't know if there
really is another name for this dish. When I lived in
Washington, DC for graduate school, I used to go to
Sunday dinner at my second cousin's home. She used
to routinely make us Aunt Rose's polenta. It was delicious!
Many usually add the cheese on top after it has finished
cooking, but I add the cheese while it's cooking.*

2	cups cold water	salt, to taste
2	cups cornmeal	pepper, to taste
3	cups boiling water	$^1/_4$–$^1/_2$ cup Parmigiano cheese

INSTRUCTIONS:

Mix cold water and cornmeal together until cornmeal absorbs water.
Gradually pour into boiling water and stir constantly over medium heat
for about 1 hour. Season to taste with salt and pepper.

Polenta will begin to pull away from sides of pan when it solidifies. Once
it does this, add the cheese and stir constantly for about 2–3 minutes.
Turn polenta out of pan onto serving dish. Sprinkle with Parmigiano
cheese.

elda's stuffing recipe

Shared by Mary Malchodi Dodd, Stamford, Connecticut

This is my grandmother Elda's stuffing recipe. She only cooked one day out of the year, but made the best Thanksgiving food ever. I have fond memories of stealing bits of stuffing when she wasn't looking! We would eat every last crumb of this stuff.

1	roll regular flavor Jimmy Dean sausage	1	large package Pepperidge Farm stuffing, irregular shaped pieces
1	cup onion, finely minced	½	teaspoon Bell's poultry seasoning
1	cup celery, chopped		salt, to taste
½	cup butter or margarine		pepper, to taste
3	Braeburn apples, peeled, cored and chopped	1	cup chicken stock, may need more for desired moistness
¾	cup walnuts, chopped		

INSTRUCTIONS:

Sauté loose sausage in frying pan until cooked and drain of all fat; reserve sausage to a bowl. In same frying pan sauté onions and celery in butter for 7 minutes. Stir in chopped apples and cook for 10 minutes. Add walnuts. Place stuffing in large bowl; add sausage, onions and celery, and seasonings. Thoroughly mix ingredients together and slowly add chicken stock to moisten and bind the stuffing.

Loosely pack stuffing in cavity of turkey until full; use heal of bread at opening to hold in place. Bake with heal of bread or lace turkey. Any excess stuffing can be baked in a buttered Pyrex dish; the deeper the glass pan the better to avoid drying out. My grandmother always stuffed the turkey, but stuffing can be prepared in a casserole dish for safety or temperature issues. All cooked stuffing should be removed as soon as the turkey comes out of the oven and has "rested" for a brief time before carving... Enjoy!

braised fennel bulbs

Shared by Black Point Inn, Prouts Neck, Scarborough, Maine

2 large fresh fennel bulbs, trimmed of tops	$^1/_3$ cup Kalamata or Niçoise black olives, with pits
2 tablespoons fruity olive oil	1 cup fresh tomato puree, strained
salt, to taste	
pepper, to taste	$^1/_2$ cup dry white wine
$^1/_2$ large yellow onion, diced	1 cup water
1 teaspoon garlic, chopped	1 teaspoon fennel seeds

INSTRUCTIONS:

Begin by splitting the fennel bulbs in half from stalk to root end, making a "V" cut to remove the core without letting the layers come apart. Heat olive oil in a thick, nonreactive roasting pan large enough to hold all 4 pieces. Salt and pepper the cut sides and brown in pan. Adjust heat to let them caramelize well, approximately 10 minutes. Reduce heat to low and add onion and garlic to sweat until translucent, 5 minutes.

Add remaining ingredients and cook, uncovered, on low heat or in the oven at 300 degrees for 40 minutes to 1 hour until the fennel is very tender. The liquid should reduce to less than half the original volume. Reserve olives and strain remaining liquid. Cut bulbs in half again. Spoon sauce over them and garnish with olives. This dish is great with salmon or lemony chicken. It works well with medium bodied red wines or any crisp white. Serves 4.

risott
(pronounced ri zut)

**Shared by Jessica Granatiero, The Savory Grape,
East Greenwich, Rhode Island**

*This recipe was that of my great aunt, Adeline Gallo,
and great, great grandmother, Raimonda Casari. Both
were Italian and lived in Pottsville, Pennsylvania.*

¹/₂	pound chicken livers, chopped	1	tablespoon Crisco oil
4	celery leaves, finely chopped	³/₄	cup raw Arborio rice
1	small onion, finely chopped	³/₄–1	cup chicken broth salt, to taste pepper, to taste Parmigiano Reggiano cheese, for topping
1	tablespoon butter		

INSTRUCTIONS:

Mix together the chicken livers, celery leaves and onion and sauté in butter and Crisco for about 5 minutes. Add the rice, chicken broth, salt and pepper to taste. Simmer slowly until rice is tender and liquid is dissolved, about 20–25 minutes. This is delicious topped with grated cheese.

asian slaw

Shared by Coffee's Country Market, Old Lyme, Connecticut

This is fantastic with our crab cakes.

DRESSING:

2	tablespoons vegetable oil	1	teaspoon fresh ginger, finely chopped
1	tablespoon fresh lime juice	1	teaspoon soy sauce
1	tablespoon rice vinegar	¼	teaspoon salt
1	teaspoon brown sugar, packed	¼	teaspoon red pepper flakes, crushed

SLAW:

3	cups green cabbage, shredded	½	cup red and yellow pepper strips, seeded, finely sliced
1	cup red cabbage, shredded		
1	cup bok choy, shredded	½	cup fresh cilantro, finely chopped
1	cup carrots, coarsely shredded	¼	cup sliced almonds, toasted
½	cup cucumber, seeded, finely sliced		

DRESSING:

Combine all ingredients and whisk together. Set aside.

SLAW:

Combine all ingredients in a large bowl. Pour dressing over and gently toss until evenly mixed. *See crab cake recipe on page 41.*

garlic green beans
with almonds

Shared by Diane Gardner, Madison, Connecticut

A family favorite.

3	cups fresh green beans		salt, to taste
3–4	cloves garlic, sliced		pepper, to taste
2	tablespoons olive oil	2	tablespoons Parmesan
1/2	cup almonds, sliced		cheese, grated

INSTRUCTIONS:

Blanch green beans until they can be pierced with a fork but are still crispy. Set aside. Sauté garlic in olive oil and as it starts to lightly brown, add almonds and sauté until golden. Add green beans and toss. Season to taste with salt and pepper and top with grated Parmesan cheese. Serve and enjoy!

rutabaga
with apple cider

Shared by Esau Crosby, Executive Chef,
Solo Bistro Bistro, Bath, Maine

1	large rutabaga or turnip, peeled and diced		pepper, to taste
	salt, to taste	3	ounces butter
		2	cups apple cider

INSTRUCTIONS:

Season rutabaga, with salt and pepper. Melt butter and sauté rutabaga until color starts to change. Add cider and simmer until vegetables are fork tender. Serves 4–6.

praline squash puree

Shared by Dyana Rudden, Branford, Connecticut

3	pounds butternut squash, peeled, seeded and cut into 1-inch chunks		pepper, to taste
		1/2	cup dark brown sugar, packed
3	eggs, lightly beaten		
1/4	teaspoon nutmeg	3/4	cup pecans, coarsely chopped
	salt, to taste	3	tablespoons butter

INSTRUCTIONS:

Boil squash in salted water, about 20 minutes or until tender. Drain and puree squash. Add eggs, nutmeg, salt and pepper. Pour into casserole. Sprinkle with brown sugar and nuts. Cut up butter and drop over the top. Bake at 375 degrees for 1/2 hour or until bubbly.

cranberry risotto

Shared by the Cape Cod Cranberry Growers' Association,
Cape Cod, Massachusetts*

2 cups cranberry juice cocktail	1 cup Arborio short grain white rice
2 tablespoons olive oil	1/4 cup feta cheese, crumbled
1/4 cup leeks, chopped	1/2 cup sweetened dried cranberries
salt, to taste	
pepper, to taste	

INSTRUCTIONS:

Pour cranberry juice into a small saucepan and place on medium-high heat. Bring to a boil. Add olive oil to 1-quart saucepan and place over high heat. Add leeks, salt and pepper. Sauté until leeks are translucent and then add rice. Stir until the rice is coated with oil.

Add the boiling cranberry juice cocktail. Stir. Cover. Turn heat down to a simmer. Let simmer for 20 minutes. Remove from heat, add feta cheese and sweetened dried cranberries, stir well. Turn into a serving dish and serve hot. Serves 8.

*Photograph courtesy of Cape Cod Cranberry Growers' Association

mother's home baked beans

Shared by Judi Mager, Westbrook, Connecticut

This is a family recipe that I have been making for 43 years and my mom made for 50 years before me. Delicious.

2 cups navy beans	1/3 cup dark molasses
4–5 pieces salt pork, chopped into 1-inch cubes	1 teaspoon vinegar
1/2 cup chili sauce	1 medium onion, chopped
2 cups hot bean liquid	1/2 teaspoon dry mustard
1 teaspoon salt	1/4 cup brown sugar

INSTRUCTIONS:

Rinse and sort beans. Cover with water, 2 inches above the beans and soak overnight. Next day simmer in covered pot (do not boil) for about 1 hour or until tender. Drain and reserve bean liquid. Cook pork cubes until brown. Pour beans into 2-quart bean pot. Add salt pork and combine remaining ingredients. Cover and bake in slow oven at 300 degrees for 6 hours. Add more bean liquid or water during cooking if necessary.

bleu cheese gratin

Shared by Formaggio Kitchen, Cambridge, Massachusetts

From our friend-chef Tony Maws.

½ pound bleu cheese, such as Fourme d'Ambert* or Persille du Pont Astier*	2 medium Yukon Gold potatoes
1 cup milk, approximately	1 tablespoon thyme, picked
5 medium russet potatoes	5 scratches fresh nutmeg
	salt, to taste
	pepper, to taste

INSTRUCTIONS:

Break cheese into chunks and place in bowl. Add ½ cup milk and using fork, mash until mixture is creamy.

Peel and rinse potatoes. Use mandolin to slice into long pieces, no more than ⅙ inch thick. Place in large bowl along with thyme, nutmeg, salt, pepper and enough milk to coat potato slices.

Butter casserole dish and season with salt and pepper. Place a layer of potato slices in the bottom, overlapping the slices in a "fish scale" pattern. Add one-third of the cheese mixture and salt and pepper the first layer. Repeat for 2 more layers, adding enough milk to barely cover the top layer of potatoes before spreading the remaining cheese mixture on top.

Cover with foil. Bake in a preheated oven of 350 degrees for 2 hours or until a sharp knife easily slides through potatoes. Uncover and bake for 20 minutes or until golden brown. Let rest for 30 minutes before slicing and serving. Serves 8.

*See reference page 307

FOURME d'AMBERT
SEMI-SOFT PASTE AND
SMOOTH TEXTURE MAKE
THIS RAW MILK BLEU
VERY VERSATILE AND
PLEASING.
THIS IS AN ANCIENT
CHEESE FROM THE
AUVERGNE REGION IN
FRANCE $12.50
LB

TRADITION
Camembert
du Bocage

250g

FABRIQUÉ EN NORMANDIE

poutines
french fries with cheese and gravy

Shared by Jason Sobocinski, Caseus Fromagerie and Bistro, New Haven, Connecticut

3	tablespoons butter		black pepper
3	tablespoons flour		peanut oil, for frying
2	cups chicken stock	8	large Idaho potatoes, sliced
1	cup cream		
	kosher salt	½	pound mozzarella curd*

INSTRUCTIONS:

VELOUTE (GRAVY):

Melt the butter in a saucepan over medium heat. Stir in flour and cook for 2 minutes.

Whisk in the stock and cream until smooth. Bring to a boil. Season with salt and pepper. Remove from heat.

POMMES FRITES (FRENCH FRIES):

Using a candy thermometer, bring oil to 300 degrees. Blanch potatoes in the hot oil for 4–5 minutes or until soft but not brown. Work in small batches as to not cool the oil down too much. Remove the potatoes and let cool to room temperature. Raise oil to 375 degrees. Cook blanched potatoes in the hot oil until browned and crispy; drain. Season with salt and pepper. Put the mozzarella curd in a safe oven dish in a medium oven until just barely melted. Remove from oven. Top with fries, then Veloute gravy.

*See reference page 307

baked sweet potato fries

Shared by Diane Gardner, Madison, Connecticut

*These are quick and easy, and kids love them. They go great
with the gingered skirt steak (page 208). Throw in a green salad
or vegetable and your meal is ready!*

3–4 sweet potatoes, peeled
and sliced French fry
style

salt, to taste

pepper, to taste

2 tablespoons rosemary,
chopped

olive oil, for drizzling

INSTRUCTIONS:

In a large bowl season potatoes with salt and pepper, rosemary and
drizzle with olive oil. Toss to coat all potatoes and spread on a cookie
sheet. Bake at 400 degrees until tender and light brown. Serves 3–4.

pesto mashed potatoes with goat cheese

Shared by Fat Toad Farm, Brookfield, Vermont

Come March, we have just about finished our supply of cider from the fall and are working on the stacks of pesto tubs, the baskets of potatoes, the whole corn waiting to be ground, and the fresh flow of all goat milk products that are filling up our fridge. This recipe is not only a practical use of many of our products but it's also a creamy delicious dinner.

5	medium size potatoes	4	ounces plain chèvre*
¼	cup goat (or cow) milk	2	tablespoons cornmeal
2	tablespoons butter	¼	cup walnuts, finely diced
4	ounces pesto	1	teaspoon salt

INSTRUCTIONS:

Boil potatoes until tender. Leave skins on and mash with milk and butter. Add other ingredients and mash or beat until thoroughly combined. Serve hot. Serves 4–5. *See reference page 307*

seafood & pasta

fettuccine alfredo with
chicken and broccoli

pasta with crabmeat sauce

shrimp parmesan

lobster with veal meatballs

lobster fra diavolo

crabmeat pie

fillet of sole vanderbilt

macaroni with sundried
tomato basil goat cheese

scalloped scallops

baked stuffed lobster

coconut salmon

d-train's penne a la vodka

seafood & pasta

bluefish cakes

baja fish tacos

lobster summer roll

betsy's smokey bolognese sauce

crème fraiche cayenne salmon

spaghetti casserole

lobster mac 'n' cheese

pan-seared scallops with
fresh corn grits

scaloppine loretta

grilled salmon with soy vinaigrette

orecchiette with sicilian
pesto and shrimp

fettuccine alfredo
with chicken and broccoli

Shared by Marisa Lonkart, Lincoln, New Hampshire

I love this recipe because it is so easy and the options are endless. I've done this with chicken, shrimp, zucchini, broccoli, and when the pantry is lean, with no meat or veggies at all. Great after a long day of skiing.

2 tablespoons olive oil	½ cup Parmesan cheese, grated
½ pound boneless chicken breasts, cut into bite size pieces	1 8-ounce package fresh linguine
salt, to taste	1 head broccoli, cut into florets
pepper, to taste	fresh Italian flat leaf parsley, for garnish
1 stick butter	
1 cup heavy cream	

INSTRUCTIONS:

Heat olive oil over medium heat in sauté pan. Season chicken with salt and pepper to taste, then sauté in olive oil until white and cooked through. Reserve on a covered platter or in a serving bowl to keep warm. In a medium heavy bottom saucepan, melt butter over low heat. Add cream and bring to simmer. Stir regularly to reduce cream, making sure not to let it boil over, about 5 minutes. Add Parmesan cheese and stir until well blended and creamy. If it gets too thick, add more cream. Cook for about 5 minutes.

Meanwhile, cook linguine according to package directions. Toss the broccoli into the pot with the linguine the last 3 minutes of cooking time. Drain and add to chicken. Pour sauce over the top of chicken mixture. Mix thoroughly. Garnish with grated Parmesan cheese and fresh parsley. Serves 2–3. Enjoy!

pasta with crabmeat sauce

Shared by Dwight Carver, Beals Island, Maine

Guys, this is simple and you just might impress the ladies!

1½–2 pounds pasta sauce, chunky garden style
for locals: crabmeat from ½ dozen good sized crabs

for Flatlanders: 1 pint fresh crabmeat

1 pound pasta, any kind, cooked

INSTRUCTIONS:

Heat pasta sauce, gently stir crabmeat into sauce and simmer for 10–15 minutes.

Pour sauce over pasta and enjoy. Serves 4.

shrimp parmesan

Shared by Andy Read, New Hampshire

spaghetti sauce

2–3 jumbo shrimp
per person

mozzarella cheese

pasta, any kind, cooked

INSTRUCTIONS:

Cover bottom of baking dish with spaghetti sauce. Butterfly shrimp and place in baking dish in a single layer. Pour additional spaghetti sauce on top of shrimp. Top with mozzarella cheese. Bake in oven at 350 degrees for 15–20 minutes. Serve over pasta.

lobster with veal meatballs

Shared by The Inn at Ocean's Edge, Lincolnville, Maine

VEAL MEATBALLS:

2	pounds ground veal	1	teaspoon red pepper, crushed
2	teaspoons dried oregano	1/3	cup cream
1/2	cup parsley, chopped	1	cup fresh bread crumbs
2	eggs	1	teaspoon salt
1/2	cup pecorino cheese, grated	1 1/2	teaspoons black pepper

INSTRUCTIONS:

Mix all ingredients together. Roll into meatballs the size of 2 tablespoons and bake until golden brown at 325 degrees.

FRESH HERB TOMATO SAUCE:

1 1/2	cups onions, chopped	1	cup V-8 juice
1/2	cup shallots, chopped	1/4	cup fresh basil, chopped
2	tablespoons garlic, chopped	3	tablespoons fresh parsley, chopped
1/4	cup olive oil	1 1/2	teaspoons fresh thyme, chopped
6	cups canned tomatoes filets	2	sage leaves, chopped
2	cups vegetable or chicken broth	1	tablespoon salt
1	cup white wine		black pepper, to taste

INSTRUCTIONS:

Sauté onions, shallots and garlic in olive oil. Add all but the herbs and simmer for 1 hour. Add the herbs, adjust seasoning to taste and puree the sauce.

1	pound fresh fettuccine	Pecorino cheese, shaved, for garnish
3	pounds fresh lobster meat, cooked and chopped in large chunks	sprig fresh basil, for garnish

INSTRUCTIONS:

Cook the pasta. Then toss with, lobster meat, meatballs and sauce and garnish with pecorino cheese and basil. Serves 4–6.

lobster fra diavolo

Shared by Bills Seafood, Westbrook, Connecticut

This is a favorite of all!

1¼ pound lobster	½ pound calamari, thinly sliced
8 cherrystone clams	16 ounces marinara sauce
12 mussels	½ teaspoon red pepper flakes
2 ounces olive oil	Tabasco sauce, to taste
2 tablespoons garlic, chopped	½ pound fettuccine or linguine, cooked
8 sea scallops	
6 medium tiger shrimp	

INSTRUCTIONS:

Put 1 inch of water in pot large enough to fit lobster and bring to a boil. Steam lobster for 10 minutes and remove. Add clams and mussels, cook until they open, discarding any that do not. Remove clams and mussels. Let the water boil down to half the amount. Strain and set aside. Cut lobster in half, remove tamale and roe (green and orange).

Place a sauté pan on medium heat with olive oil. Cook garlic for 2 minutes while stirring. Add liquid from lobster and bring to simmer. Add scallops, shrimp and calamari and cook 2–3 minutes. Add marinara, red pepper flakes, Tabasco, lobster, mussels and clams. Simmer slowly for 5–6 minutes. Arrange over pasta and spoon the sauce over everything. Serves 1–2.

crabmeat pie

Shared by Sanders Fish Market, Portsmouth, New Hampshire

This is one of Sanders signature dishes. It's a snap to put together and extremely satisfying to eat. As the saying goes, this recipe is "as easy as pie". This is a favorite of the teachers and staff at Portsmouth's Little Harbour School.

3 tablespoons mayonnaise	8 ounces fresh crabmeat*
2 eggs, beaten	2 scallions, sliced, optional
1 tablespoon flour	1 unbaked pie crust
1/4 teaspoon garlic powder	paprika, for garnish
1/2 pound Swiss cheese, grated	

INSTRUCTIONS:

Whisk together mayonnaise, eggs, flour and garlic powder. Gently fold in cheese, crabmeat and scallions, beating well. Pour mixture into pie crust, spreading evenly to cover bottom. Sprinkle a light dusting of paprika over top for color. Bake at 350 degrees for 35–40 minutes. Serves 4–6.

*See reference page 307

fillet of sole vanderbilt

Shared by Brick Alley Pub and Restaurant, Newport, Rhode Island

This is an original recipe that has been on our menu since our doors opened in 1980. It is a favorite of locals and tourists alike.

4	tablespoons garlic butter	1/2	pound Monterey Jack cheese, grated
8	fresh sole fillets	1	cup hollandaise sauce
1/2	pound bay scallops		parsley, chopped
1/4	pound snow crabmeat		paprika, for sprinkling
1/4	pound mushrooms, sliced and sautéed		

INSTRUCTIONS:

Preheat oven to 425 degrees. Butter the bottom of 4 individual casserole dishes with 1 tablespoon of garlic butter each. Place 1 sole fillet on the bottom and layer with a quarter of the scallops, crabmeat and mushrooms, then top with cheese. Place a second fillet on the top of each casserole and top each with 2 tablespoons of hollandaise sauce. Place in oven and bake until the fish is flaky and the sauce bubbles, about 12–15 minutes. Top each portion with the remainder of the hollandaise sauce and sprinkle lightly with parsley and paprika. Serve immediately. Serves 4.

macaroni
with sundried tomato basil goat cheese

Shared by Fat Toad Farm, Brookfield, Vermont

1	pound spiral or elbow pasta	8	ounces cheddar cheese, grated
5	tablespoons unsalted butter	8	ounces sundried tomato basil chèvre*
6	tablespoons flour		bread crumbs, for sprinkling on top
2	teaspoons dry mustard		fresh basil leaves, for garnish
5	cups goat or cow milk		

INSTRUCTIONS:

Cook pasta until just tender; drain. In a pan, melt butter over medium heat until it foams. Add flour and mustard and whisk until combined. Continue whisking for an additional minute. Slowly add the milk while whisking. Bring this mixture to a boil. Decrease heat to medium-low, whisking occasionally. Simmer until mixture thickens. Take the mixture off the heat and add both cheeses, stirring until melted. Add this mixture to the pasta and cook for about 5 minutes over medium heat. Pour mixture into a 13 x 9 baking dish. Sprinkle with bread crumbs. Broil until golden brown; about 5 minutes. Garnish with basil leaves.

*See reference page 307

scalloped scallops

Shared by CW Shellfish, Guilford, Connecticut

*When we get fresh sea scallops, this is the tastiest
way to use them.*

3/4	cup unsalted butter	1 1/2–2	pounds fresh scallops
2	cups Ritz cracker crumbs	1 1/2	cups light cream
1	cup plain bread crumbs	2	teaspoons paprika
			salt, to taste
			pepper, to taste

INSTRUCTIONS:

Preheat oven to 350 degrees. Grease a 1 1/2 or 2-quart casserole dish.
Melt butter over low heat and add cracker and bread crumbs to moisten.
Sprinkle one third of crumbs over the bottom of the dish; top with half
of the scallops. Pour half of the cream over the scallops and sprinkle
with salt and pepper. Layer on another third of the crumbs, followed by
the rest of the scallops and cream. Season again with salt and pepper.
Top with remaining bread crumbs and sprinkle with paprika. Bake until
just cooked through and bubbling, 30–40 minutes. Serves 4–6.

baked stuffed lobster

Shared by Richard Walston, Guilford, Connecticut

We go to our house on Beals Island in Maine where the lobster, scallops and crabmeat are plentiful. Just ask and you will receive. Our friends the fishermen stop by and drop off whatever we need. This local and fresh off the boat seafood makes the best baked stuffed lobster. Go ahead and be brave, add the tamale (lobster liver) to the stuffing; that is what makes it so GOOD!

4	1¼–1½ pound lobsters
1	pound sea scallops
2	sleeves Ritz crackers, crushed
1	pint fresh crabmeat
1	stick unsalted butter, melted
	tamale (the green liver) from the cavity of the lobster

INSTRUCTIONS:

This is the toughest part for some people but it has got to be done. Lay each lobster on its back and take a sharp, stiff knife and place it by the mouth. Push the blade down and cut from the mouth straight down to the tail, being careful not to cut through the shell. Use a small mallet or the butt end of a knife and lightly pound the claw so it cracks, not breaks but cracks so that it will cook evenly with the rest of the lobster. Clean out the guts in the cavity, and the vein in the tail. Take out the tamale and keep it aside.

Slice scallops side to side and lay them inside the lobster cavity down to the tip of the tail. In a bowl, add the Ritz crumbs with the crabmeat and the tamale and make it into a stuffing. Lightly pack the cavity with the stuffing, covering the scallops, and continue to add stuffing to the tip of the tail.

Spoon the melted butter over the stuffing. Pour ½ cup of water into the bottom of the pan and cover with foil. Bake 20–25 minutes on 450 degrees, then take off the foil and put lobsters under the broiler for 5 minutes until the stuffing is crisp and browned. Serves 4.

coconut salmon

Shared by Marlon Lindsay, West Hartford, Connecticut

This is a killer recipe. It's Amanda's and my favorite dish and the kids love it, too. An original recipe from my dinner table.

3	pounds salmon		salt, to taste
	vinegar or lemon juice, for washing salmon	1	large onion, diced
		2	cloves garlic, chopped
	garlic powder, to taste		vegetable oil
	onion powder, to taste	1	large tomato, diced
	black pepper, to taste	1	can Goya or Grace coconut milk
1/2	teaspoon fresh thyme, chopped		

INSTRUCTIONS:

Wash salmon in vinegar or lemon juice to cut the fishy smell and taste. Slice into 2–3 inch pieces. In a bowl or large plastic bag, sprinkle salmon with garlic powder, onion powder, pepper, thyme and salt, generously covering each piece. Slice onion and garlic and add to the seasoned salmon. Mix and let sit for 30 minutes.

Heat oil in frying pan on medium heat. Remove salmon and brown on both sides until slightly crispy. Place salmon on paper towels to drain.

Pour out the oil, but do not wash the pan. Place back on stove and add onion, garlic and tomatoes. Sauté until onions are soft. Stir in coconut milk. Add salmon. Use 1 cup of water to rinse the bowl or bag to get the excess seasoning out and add this to fry pan or pot. Let simmer, covered, on medium heat until it thickens, about 20 minutes. Watch to make sure it does not burn. Serve over rice, potatoes or boiled dumplings. Enjoy. Serves 4–6.

d-train's penne
a la vodka

Shared by D-Train's Foods, Westbrook, Connecticut

1 medium onion, finely
chopped

¹/₂ stick unsalted butter

²/₃ cup vodka

³/₄ cup tomato puree

1 cup heavy cream

¹/₄ pound cooked ham,
finely chopped

2 tablespoons D-Train's
hot pepper sauce*

¹/₂ teaspoon salt

¹/₄ teaspoon black pepper

1 pound penne, cooked
al dente, reserve ¹/₂ cup
water

³/₄ cup Parmigiano Reggiano
cheese, grated

INSTRUCTIONS:

Cook onion in butter in a deep 12-inch heavy skillet over moderate-low heat, stirring occasionally. Stir in vodka and simmer for 4 minutes. Add tomato puree and cream; simmer for another 5 minutes. Stir in ham, hot sauce, salt and pepper. Add cooked pasta to sauce and toss. If dry, add a little of reserved water from pasta. Top with grated cheese and give another toss. Serve immediately. Serves 4.

*See reference page 307

bluefish cakes
"not my dad's fish cakes"

Shared by Scott Woodford, Madison, Connecticut

2 pieces bluefish, white meat only	salt, to taste
	pepper, to taste
handful Pepperidge Farm stuffing mix	1–2 cloves garlic, crushed
1–2 eggs	olive oil, for sautéing, or butter
curry, to taste	baby greens

INSTRUCTIONS:

Dice fish into chunks, removing all colored flesh. Add Pepperidge Farm stuffing mix to bind with fish. Mix eggs in a bowl, then add gently to fish mixture, just enough to bind all ingredients together. Season to taste with curry, salt, pepper and garlic. Form fish cakes and sauté in olive oil until golden brown on each side.

Place fish cakes over a bed of baby greens and drizzle with wasabi sauce. Serve and enjoy!

DRESSING:

1 cup mayonnaise	2 tablespoons pickled ginger, finely chopped
wasabi paste, to taste	milk, for desired consistency

INSTRUCTIONS:

Mix mayonnaise with wasabi to the desired flavor. Add ginger and milk to make a thick pouring dressing.

baja fish tacos

Shared by Stephen Dewey, Chatham Fish and Lobster,
Chatham, Massachusetts

FISH TACOS:

1   pound cod, cut into
    ¹/₂–³/₄ inch thick strips*

    corn flour or cornmeal,
    for dredging

    evaporated milk

    canola or vegetable oil,
    for frying

4   6-inch tortillas

    cabbage, shredded

    cilantro, picked leaves

    fresh lime juice

INSTRUCTIONS:

Preheat oven to 350 degrees. Place strips of fish into corn flour, then into evaporated milk, then back into corn flour. Drop fish into oil and allow to cook. They are done when they float. Remove from oil and place on a paper towel to drain excess oil.

Warm flour tortillas in the microwave for 10–15 seconds; keep covered. Place a fish in the center of each tortilla. Top with cabbage, cilantro leaves, guacamole, chipotle sour cream and fresh lime juice. Enjoy!

GUACAMOLE:

2   ripe avocados

    red onion, diced, to taste

1   tomato, seeded and diced

    fresh lime juice, to taste

    salt, to taste

INSTRUCTIONS:

Cut avocados and remove seeds. Place avocado flesh in bowl and mash. Add diced onion and tomatoes. Squeeze in lime juice and add salt to taste. Mix and serve.

CHIPOTLE SOUR CREAM:

    sour cream

    chipotle chili powder,
    to taste

    fresh lime juice, to taste

INSTRUCTIONS:

Put desired amount of sour cream in a bowl. Add chipotle chili powder to taste. Squeeze in fresh lime to taste. Mix well.

*See reference page 307

lobster summer roll
with yuzo cashew dipping sauce

Shared by Chef Anthony Cole, Chatham Bars Inn,
Chatham, Massachusetts

SUMMER ROLLS:

rice paper wrappers
basil, rolled and chopped
mint, rolled and chopped
cooked lobster meat

Granny Smith apples,
julienned
Enoki mushrooms
cucumbers, peeled and
julienned

INSTRUCTIONS:

Soak rice paper in warm water. Cut into 4 pieces by first cutting across and then diagonal.

Place basil, mint and lobster down on one quarter each of the soaked wrapper. Next add apple, mushroom, cucumber. Roll in a cone shape and store under a damp paper towel before serving with dipping sauce.

DIPPING SAUCE:

¼ cup sweet soy sauce
¼ cup Kikkoman's teriyaki sauce
2 tablespoons yuzo
2 tablespoons fish sauce
2 tablespoons sesame seed oil
2 tablespoons sterling salad oil

2 tablespoons rice wine vinegar
1 teaspoon Kafir lime leaf, finely minced
1 cup unsalted cashews, lightly toasted and chopped
2 teaspoons cilantro, finely chopped

INSTRUCTIONS:

Combine all ingredients.

betsy's smokey bolognese sauce

Shared by Betsy Rudden, Farmington, Connecticut

This recipe has evolved over the years. It is a combination of two great recipes, one from my best friend's mom, Inez, and the other from my friend Amy. As I usually do, I try to improve upon the original, hence the addition of the bacon and smoked paprika and cream, my own special twist.

My family loves when I make this and it is very easy to prepare. The sauce is ready to eat in an hour and a half, but if you leave it to cool and then serve it the next day, it's even better. It also freezes well. I use a large enameled cast iron pan which distributes the heat evenly.

6	large cloves garlic, chopped	2	28 ounce cans crushed tomatoes
	olive oil	1	28 ounce can diced tomatoes with roasted garlic
3	pounds ground pork		
1/2	pound bacon cut into 1 inch pieces, optional	1	smoked ham hock
	salt, to taste	1	cup half and half
	pepper, to taste	1/2	cup Parmesan cheese
2	tablespoons smoked paprika	1	pound linguine, cooked

INSTRUCTIONS:

Sauté garlic in olive oil, being careful not to burn. Add pork in 3 batches and brown well. Transfer to a bowl after each batch, discarding the excess fat. Once all of the pork is cooked, break apart by hand so that there are no clumps. Add more olive oil if needed. In the same pan, sauté the bacon until very crisp and set aside. Drain the bacon grease and discard.

Still using the same pan, pour a bit more olive oil to gloss the bottom. Add the cooked pork and season with salt, pepper and the smoked paprika. Stir in the tomatoes, place the smoked ham hock in the center of the sauce, and cover the pan. Simmer for 40 minutes. Add additional salt, pepper and paprika to taste.

Remove the ham hock and discard. Add the half and half and cheese and stir. Sauté for another 15 minutes with the cover off. Add the crisp bacon and serve over linguine.

crème fraiche cayenne salmon

Shared by Allison Wolf, Vermont Butter and Cheese Company, Websterville, Vermont

4   pieces salmon fillets,
    ½ pound each

¼   cup white wine

1   shallot, chopped
    salt, to taste

pepper, to taste

4   teaspoons cayenne pepper

4   tablespoons Vermont
    crème fraiche*

INSTRUCTIONS:

Preheat broiler. Place salmon and wine in shallow baking dish. Garnish with chopped shallot, salt, pepper and cayenne. Spread crème fraiche on top of salmon. Place under broiler in the low part of the oven and cook for 20–25 minutes. Serve with basmati rice and green beans or blanched asparagus sautéed in Vermont sea salt butter. Serves 4.

*See reference page 307

spaghetti casserole

Shared by Dottie Stawarky, Westbrook, Connecticut

1 pound angel hair pasta, al dente	1/2 pound ground beef
2 eggs	1/2 pound ground sausage
1/2 cup Parmesan cheese	1 small onion, thinly sliced
1 pound ricotta cheese or cottage cheese spaghetti sauce	1 small green pepper, thinly sliced
	8 ounces mozzarella cheese

INSTRUCTIONS:

In a 9 x 15 pan, form a crust by layering the angel hair pasta on the bottom. Mix the eggs with the Parmesan cheese and stir into the pasta. Spread the ricotta cheese on top of the crust.

Meanwhile, cook the beef, sausage, onions and green peppers. Stir in spaghetti sauce. Layer the casserole with the meat mixture. Cover with foil and bake for 30 minutes at 350 degrees. Uncover and sprinkle with mozzarella cheese and bake for another 10 minutes or until the cheese melts. Heat remaining sauce and serve on the side. Serves 3–4.

lobster mac 'n' cheese

Shared by Sanders Fish Market, Portsmouth, New Hampshire

This recipe was created for Christmas 2007 and was a huge hit. It is a comfort food that is both deeply satisfying and elegant at the same time.

2	pounds fresh lobster meat, cut into chunks*		8	ounces Gruyère cheese, grated
1	large Vidalia onion, diced		8	ounces Parmesan cheese, grated
2	tablespoons butter		8	ounces low-fat cream cheese
4	cloves garlic, minced			
6	tablespoons flour		1	pound Barilla large shells, cooked al dente
6	tablespoons butter			
4½	cups skim milk		½	cup Panko bread crumbs
2	teaspoons Better than Bouillon lobster base		2	teaspoons paprika
10	ounces Cracker Barrel extra sharp yellow cheddar cheese, grated		2	teaspoons dried parsley, optional

INSTRUCTIONS:

Cook lobster; set aside.

In a large pot, sauté onions in 2 tablespoons butter until translucent. Add minced garlic and cook a minute longer. Stir in 6 tablespoons flour and 6 tablespoons butter to make a roux. Add milk and lobster base and whisk until thickened.

Whisk in cheese until melted and smooth. Fold in shells and lobster meat. Pour mixture into buttered 4 quart baking dish. Sprinkle top with mixture of Panko and paprika. Bake in preheated oven at 350 degrees for 30–45 minutes until bubbly and lightly browned. Do not overcook. Serves 10–12.

*See reference page 307

pan-seared scallops
with fresh corn grits

Shared by Chef Anthony Cole,
Chatham Bars Inn, Chatham, Massachusetts

CORN GRITS:

4	ears sweet corn	2	ounces heavy cream
2	tablespoons shallots, minced	¼	cup Parmesan cheese, grated
2	tablespoons butter		salt, to taste

INSTRUCTIONS:

Grate corn ears. In a medium saucepan, sauté shallots with butter on medium-low heat until translucent. Add corn and heavy cream. Simmer on low heat for 5 minutes. Add cheese and salt to taste. Keep warm.

SEARED SCALLOPS:

6	large scallops	1	tablespoon unsalted butter
	salt, to taste		
	pepper, to taste	2	sprigs fresh thyme
1	tablespoon salad oil		

INSTRUCTIONS:

Preheat 12-inch cast iron pan on medium-high heat. Season scallops. Heat oil over medium-high heat. Place scallops in pan, sear the first side until brown, then turn and add butter and thyme. As butter melts, baste scallops with butter. Serve warm grits in a bowl and top with scallops.

scaloppine loretta

Shared by Sardella's Restaurant, Newport, Rhode Island

*This dish is named after Richard Sardella's mother.
It was her recipe and upon her passing, it was added
to the menu. Every time family members visit
the restaurant, they are sure to order the Veal Loretta.
It is also one of our more popular dishes.*

12	veal medallions, ¼ inch thick	2	ounces onions, julienned
	salt, to taste	4	ounces pancetta, sliced
	pepper, to taste	2	ounces mushrooms, sliced
	flour, for dusting medallions	2	ounces brandy
		6	ounces veal stock
2	tablespoons olive oil	2	tablespoons butter
		1	pound linguine, cooked

INSTRUCTIONS:

Season medallions with salt and pepper; dust with flour. In a medium saucepan, over moderately high heat, add olive oil. Sauté the medallions for 2 minutes per side. Remove from the pan to complete the sauce. Add onions and pancetta, sauté until transparent, then add the mushrooms and the veal medallions. Flame with brandy and add veal stock and butter. Reduce for 2 minutes. Serve over linguine. Serves 2.

grilled salmon
with soy vinaigrette

**Shared by Stephen Dewey, Chatham Fish and Lobster,
Chatham, Massachusetts**

2	tablespoons Dijon mustard	6	tablespoons extra virgin olive oil
1/2	teaspoon garlic, minced	2	pounds fresh salmon*
3	tablespoons low-sodium soy sauce	1	tablespoon olive oil

INSTRUCTIONS:

Whisk together the mustard, garlic and soy sauce. Then drizzle the olive oil in while whisking to emulsify. Set aside. Preheat the grill, oil the fish and place it flesh down. Let it cook for 5–6 minutes on the first side, depending on thickness. Then flip it over and cook for a few minutes. Slip a metal spatula in between the skin and flesh and slide the skin off. Allow the fish to finish cooking to the desired doneness. Drizzle with the soy vinaigrette. Serve over jasmine rice. Serves 3–4.

*See reference page 307

orecchiette with sicilian pesto and shrimp

**Shared by Russell Vito, Chef,
The Guilford Bistro and Grille Café, Guilford, Connecticut**

*I am chef and co-owner of the Guilford Bistro. I studied in
Sicily, and bring this authentic dish to you. Enjoy!*

olive oil, for sautéing

1   shallot, diced

5   shrimp, peeled

½   cup fresh spinach

1   roasted red pepper, diced
    salt, to taste

pepper, to taste

2   cups fresh tomato sauce

½   cup basil pesto

1½ cups orecchiette pasta,
    cooked al dente

INSTRUCTIONS:

Heat olive oil in pan and sauté shallot; add shrimp and season with salt
and pepper. Add spinach and roasted red peppers, season to taste. Sauté
all together, then add tomato sauce and basil pesto. Let heat and add
cooked pasta and toss.

dinners

gingered skirt steak

easy chicken pie

apricot pork tenderloin

di's pulled pork

stuffed chicken

chicken and dumplings

easy chicken

almond chicken breast with pears

veal, sausage and peppers

peppered pork roast

vermont maple berry chicken

meat pie

rabbit saltimbocca

dinners

ale braised short ribs

rhonda's "nonna's" eggplant parmesan

norris granatiero meatloaf

coq au vin

black watch farm meatloaf

chicken florentine

perlow southern style

beef stew provencal

lamb leg steak

mom's pot roast

simon's meatloaf

gingered skirt steak

Shared by Diane Gardner, Madison, Connecticut

*This is a family favorite in all seasons, but especially
in the summer on the grill. Easy and delicious,
great for a big family bar-be-cue!*

1¹/₂–2   pounds skirt steak   pepper, to taste
         (about 3 pieces)   crushed red pepper
³/₄   cup soy sauce   flakes, to taste
¹/₃   cup fresh ginger,
         chopped

INSTRUCTIONS:

Marinate skirt steak in soy and ginger, season with pepper and red
pepper flakes, shake well. Cover and refrigerate overnight or at least let
marinate all day. Grill about 2–3 minutes per side and let rest for 5 minutes
before slicing. Slice on the diagonal. Serve immediately. Serves 3–4 for
dinner or 8–10 for appetizer.

easy chicken pie

Shared by Fran Gardner, Florence, South Carolina

3 1/2 pounds chicken,
    cooked until tender

2–3 eggs, boiled

2 1/2 cups chicken stock

1 can cream of
    chicken soup

salt, to taste

pepper, to taste

INSTRUCTIONS:

Debone chicken and place in bottom of dish. Dice eggs and put on top of chicken. Mix chicken stock and soup together and heat. Pour this mixture over the chicken and eggs. Season with salt and pepper.

TOPPING:

1 cup self-rising flour

1 cup buttermilk

1 stick margarine or butter, melted

INSTRUCTIONS:

Mix all together and pour over top of chicken pie. Bake at 425 degrees for 25–30 minutes. Delicious! Serves 4–6.

apricot pork tenderloin

Shared by Joan Dunham, Westbrook, Connecticut

1½ pounds pork tenderloin
¼ cup olive oil
2 cloves garlic, minced
   cracked black
   peppercorns, to taste

salt, to taste
½ cup triple sec
   dried apricots

INSTRUCTIONS:

Marinate pork in olive oil, garlic, pepper and salt for 5–6 hours. Place tenderloin in shallow roasting pan. Add triple sec and scatter dried apricots around meat.

Roast for 20 minutes at 450 degrees, lower the heat to 350 degrees and bake for another 20 minutes. Sliced apples may be used.

di's pulled pork

Shared by Diane Gardner, Madison, Connecticut

1 4–5 pound pork picnic
   shoulder, bone in
   kosher salt, to taste
   coarsely ground black
   pepper, to taste
3–4 tablespoons olive oil

1½–2 cups vinegar
2 large boxes chicken
   broth
   red pepper flakes, to
   taste

INSTRUCTIONS:

Rinse pork shoulder and generously rub in kosher salt and pepper. Heat olive oil in Dutch oven on top of stove at medium-high heat. Sear all sides of shoulder until nice and brown. Remove from stove and add vinegar and enough broth to cover up to two-thirds of the shoulder. Sprinkle with red pepper flakes to taste. Bake in a 250–275 degree oven for 8–10 hours. Baste every so often to keep moist. When it's tender, it just pulls apart and it's delicious.

stuffed chicken
petti di pollo romano

Shared by Sardella's Restaurant, Newport, Rhode Island

*This has been on the menu since 1980. It was created
by Richard Sardella for a group of friends who came
in weekly and wanted something different that they had
never had before. This was the result and continues
to be a local favorite.*

2	8-ounce boneless chicken breasts	1	tablespoon unsalted butter
12	ounces mozzarella cheese, shredded	1/4	cup all purpose flour
1	teaspoon garlic, diced	1/4	cup dry white wine
2	ounces fresh parsley, chopped	1/2	cup chicken broth
1/4	cup olive oil		salt, to taste
			pepper, to taste
		1/2	pound linguine, cooked

INSTRUCTIONS:

Cut chicken breasts in half and trim off any fat. Using a meat mallet, pound each half to 1/8 inch thick. Set aside.

In a small bowl, mix mozzarella, garlic and parsley. Add a drizzle of olive oil to bind the mixture. By hand, roll the mixture into 4 equal size balls. Place the balls in the center of each piece of chicken and roll the chicken around each ball. Use toothpicks to seal each breast.

Preheat oven to 375 degrees. Flour each chicken breast and pat off any excess flour. Set the chicken aside after seasoning to taste. Heat a 12-inch sauté pan over high heat for 2–3 minutes. Add the olive oil and butter. When the oil and butter are hot, add each chicken breast to the pan. Brown on each side, about 3 minutes. When the chicken is brown, add the white wine and chicken broth and let the excess alcohol burn off, about 2 minutes.

Place the skillet in the preheated oven for 3–5 minutes. The chicken will puff up. Remove from the oven and place the chicken over linguine and divide the sauce equally. Serves 2.

chicken and dumplings

Shared by DiGrazia Vineyards, Brookfield, Connecticut

A hearty dinner for a cold winter evening. Enjoy!

3	split chicken breasts, bone in	4	cups chicken broth
1/4	cup butter or margarine	1	teaspoon sugar
1/2	cup onion, chopped	1	teaspoon salt
1/4	cup celery, chopped	1	teaspoon pepper
2	tablespoons celery leaves, chopped	1	teaspoon basil leaves
	garlic, minced, to taste	3	bay leaves
1/4	cup flour	1/4	cup parsley, chopped
		1	10-ounce bag frozen peas

BASIL DUMPLINGS:

2 cups Bisquick mix

1 teaspoon basil leaves

2/3 cup milk

INSTRUCTIONS:

Brown chicken in butter; remove chicken and add onion, celery, celery leaves and garlic to skillet, cooking until vegetables are tender. Sprinkle with flour and mix well. Add chicken broth, sugar, salt, pepper, basil, bay leaves and parsley; bring to boiling, stirring constantly. Place chicken in a heavy Dutch oven, pour sauce over it, cover and cook in a 350 degree oven for 40 minutes.

Combine dumpling ingredients and stir with a fork until dough is formed. Remove chicken from oven; turn heat to 425 degrees. Stir peas into the Dutch oven mixture. Drop dumplings onto stew. Return to 425 degree oven and cook, uncovered, 10 minutes; cover and cook for 10 more minutes or until chicken is tender and dumplings are done. Serves 6.

easy chicken

Shared by Andy Read, New Hampshire

3	boneless, skinless chicken breasts, halved or cut into bite size pieces	1	can cream of chicken soup
1	package Swiss cheese, sliced	¹/₂	cup white wine stuffing mix
	fresh mushrooms, sliced	4–5	tablespoons butter, melted, for drizzling

INSTRUCTIONS:

Place chicken breasts in baking dish. Place Swiss cheese on top. Cover with mushrooms. Combine chicken soup with wine and pour over the top. Layer with stuffing mix. Drizzle melted butter on top and bake at 350 degrees for 45 minutes.

almond crusted chicken breast with pears

Shared by Carol Kenyhercz, Branford, Connecticut

4	boneless, skinless chicken breasts flour, for dredging	2	tablespoons shallots, minced
1	egg, beaten	1	small pear, peeled and sliced
3/4	cup almonds, finely crushed	1/4	cup white cooking wine
2	tablespoons olive oil	1/4	cup heavy cream
			salt, to taste
			pepper, to taste

INSTRUCTIONS:

Dredge chicken in flour, then egg, coat in almonds. Heat oil in skillet; cook chicken, turning once, 4–6 minutes per side. Put chicken on ovenproof platter and keep chicken heated in a 200 degree oven. Add shallots to skillet, sauté and add pear slices. Cook over moderate heat until glazed. Add the wine and reduce by half. Reduce heat, stir in heavy cream, salt and pepper to taste. Place chicken on plate and top with pear mixture.

veal, sausage and peppers

Shared by Marisa Lonkart, Narragansett, Rhode Island

This is a version of a dish my Italian grandmother used to make. Even after years of my making it, it never comes out quite as good as hers did! Make sure you have lots of crusty Italian bread to dip into the sauce. For sandwich lovers, this is also good in a crusty Italian roll.

1 pound Italian sausage, cut into bite size pieces

2 sticks butter, approximately olive oil

1 pound veal stew meat, fat trimmed, cut into bite size pieces

salt, to taste

pepper, to taste

3 red bell peppers, sliced

1 pound mushrooms, halved

1 29-ounce can Hunt's sauce

INSTRUCTIONS:

In a sauté pan large enough to ultimately hold all of the above ingredients, cook the sausage on medium heat. Color should be good on all sides, inside does not need to be cooked through, as sausage will be combined with all ingredients at the end and simmered to complete the cooking process.

If sausage is too lean and does not yield any fat, add equal parts butter and olive oil to the pan. Remove cooked sausage to a bowl. Season veal pieces with salt and pepper and cook in butter in the same pan until no longer pink. Remove and add to sausage bowl.

Season peppers with salt and pepper and cook in plenty of butter in the same pan for about 3–4 minutes, until colored but still firm. Add to sausage and veal. Now season the mushrooms with salt and pepper and cook in a generous amount of butter. Add to the other cooked ingredients in the bowl.

Put Hunt's sauce with 3 tablespoons of butter into the hot pan and scrape the bottom with a wooden spoon to remove all the bits and flavor from the bottom. Add all cooked ingredients back into the sauce and combine. Once the mixture begins to bubble, turn the heat down and simmer, covered, for at least 30 minutes, stirring occasionally. Drizzle with olive oil before serving with lots of crusty Italian bread. Serves 4. Enjoy!

peppered pork roast

Shared by Fran Gardner, Florence, South Carolina

4–5 pound pork roast*

black pepper, to taste
salt, to taste

INSTRUCTIONS:

Rub black pepper on top and bottom of roast. Do not be stingy with the pepper. Wrap roast in Saran wrap and refrigerate for 2 days. Remove Saran wrap and wrap in foil. Cook 30 minutes per pound. When roast is almost finished baking, open the foil and let the top of roast brown. Add salt to taste when ready to serve.

The butt roast or shoulder has more fat and therefore gives much more flavor and makes the roast juicier.

vermont maple berry chicken

Shared by John Reagan, Dot's Diner, Wilmington, Vermont

6	6-ounce boneless, skinless chicken breasts	1	cup pure Vermont maple syrup
3	cups mixed blueberries, strawberries, blackberries and raspberries	1	cup white wine, optional

INSTRUCTIONS:

Grill or pan fry chicken breast about 4–5 minutes per side on medium heat. Add nonstick spray to a separate sauté pan. Over medium heat add berries and maple syrup. As the mixture reduces, add wine and continue reduction until it becomes a syrupy sauce. Add cooked chicken during last minute of reduction and serve. Serves 6.

meat pie
mémère's boudreau toutiere

Shared by Sarah Galluzzo, Fairfield, Connecticut

3 pounds ground pork

1 pound ground beef

1 large onion, chopped

salt, to taste

pepper, to taste

1 teaspoon sage

1 teaspoon poultry seasoning (use extra sage if you do not have poultry seasoning)

1 teaspoon cinnamon

1 teaspoon nutmeg

1 cup water

1 can beef broth

1 package Pepperidge Farm stuffing

2 cups instant potato flakes

2 unbaked pie crusts

egg white, beaten

INSTRUCTIONS:

Put meat, onions and seasonings in large pan with water and broth. Cook for about 1/2 hour; beef will turn brown before pork. Add all seasonings and mix, then add stuffing and potatoes and cook another 20 minutes or so.

Pour into pie crust and top with crust brushed with egg white and salt. Bake at 350 degrees for about one hour or till crust is golden. ENJOY!

rabbit saltimbocca

**Shared by Wesley Babb, Burdick's Post Office Café,
Walpole, New Hampshire**

*Our take on a traditional veal dish uses rabbit, which is
plentiful in our area. We have a rabbit farm in Dummerston,
Vermont, that raises rabbits using organic feed and delivers
twice monthly. This dish is a favorite among our clientele.*

4	rabbit tenderloins*		salt, to taste
6	sprigs sage		pepper, to taste
8	slices prosciutto, thinly sliced	2	tablespoons canola oil
1/4	cup Cognac	3	cups chicken stock, reduced by half

INSTRUCTIONS:

Flay open the rabbit so the tenderloin is as thin as the belly. Cut each tenderloin in half; put a few sage leaves on each. Top with a slice of prosciutto and pound with meat tenderizer to tenderize as well as to fuse the tenderloin to the prosciutto.

In a hot sauté pan, add canola oil and sear the prosciutto side until the ham is crisp; then turn over the cutlets and allow the rabbit to just cook through. Remove from the pan and deglaze with Cognac, taking care not to set the house on fire!! Add salt and pepper to taste and chicken stock and allow to simmer until the sauce thickens.

Serve the cutlets with broccoli rabe and fingerling potatoes, or with whipped potato and vegetables.

I was unable to find rabbit, so I substituted pork tenderloin and it was delicious.

black watch farm ale braised short ribs

Shared by Frank Manafort, Springfield, Vermont

6	pounds Black Watch Farm short ribs*	9	cloves garlic
	salt, to taste	4	cups low sodium beef broth
	black pepper, to taste	1	16-ounce can organic tomatoes, roasted
	canola oil, for sautéing		
3	cups medium bodied ale	1 1/2	teaspoons fresh rosemary, chopped
3	large onions, medium diced	1	tablespoon fresh thyme, chopped
2	carrots, medium diced		
4	small potatoes, medium diced	3	bay leaves
		1/4	cup all purpose flour
1	small turnip, small diced		

INSTRUCTIONS:

Start by seasoning each rib with salt and black pepper. Heat a cast iron skillet with canola oil until very hot. Place ribs in bone side up and sear until each rib is golden brown. Remove ribs from pan and let it cool for a couple of minutes. Place ribs into pan deep enough to submerge ribs. Meanwhile deglaze skillet with the beer. Pour deglazing liquid and all other ingredients except flour over ribs. Cover pan with foil and place ribs into a 275 degree oven. Cook for several hours. To test, place a knife into thickest part of the rib and twist. If knife twists easily, then the ribs are done. Or use the old classic method; if they are starting to fall off the bone, then they are ready. Strain liquid from ribs into a saucepan and bring back to a boil. Add flour, stirring constantly until thickened and the flour has cooked out. Season with salt and pepper and enjoy. Serve with buttered noodles. Serves 6.

See reference page 307

rhonda's "nonna's" eggplant parmesan

Shared by Rhonda Marsala, Branford, Connecticut

This is my childhood favorite! My Nonna's recipe...

EGGPLANT:

2	large eggplants, skin removed
	salt, for removing bitters
2	eggs
	flour, for dredging
	olive oil, for frying

SAUCE:

5	cloves garlic, finely chopped
2	cans Cento tomatoes, crushed
3	basil leaves, chopped
1	small can tomato paste
1	carrot, for reducing acidity
1/4	cup Parmesan Reggiano cheese
	mozzarella cheese or ricotta cheese

INSTRUCTIONS:

Slice eggplants into thin cutlets and lightly salt to take out the bitters. Let sit for a while and then pat dry. Mix 2 eggs in medium bowl. Dredge eggplant in flour and then in egg batter.

Using a frying pan, heat a thin layer of oil to medium heat and place eggplant in pan. Cook until golden brown. Repeat until all eggplant is cooked.

Sauté garlic. Add remaining ingredients and simmer 1–3 hours. Remove carrot.

Using a rectangular dish, coat with tomato sauce and layer eggplant, then sauce, then Parmesan cheese, repeating until casserole dish is filled. Sprinkle the last layer with mozzarella cheese and cover with foil. Bake at 350 degrees for 25 minutes.

norris granatiero meatloaf

Shared by Jessica Granatiero, The Savory Grape, East Greenwich, Rhode Island

This meatloaf has evolved throughout the history of our family, and I have changed it to make what my family calls the best, most moist meatloaf. Enjoy!

1/2	pound ground hamburger	1/2	cup Parmigiano Reggiano cheese
1/2	pound ground veal	1	onion, chopped
1/2	pound ground pork	1	clove garlic, chopped
1/2	cup rolled oats	3	eggs, slightly beaten by hand
1/2	cup Italian bread crumbs	1	teaspoon oregano
1/2–2/3	cup ketchup		salt, to taste
			pepper, to taste

INSTRUCTIONS:

Combine all the above ingredients together by hand. Do not over mix. Place in a large loaf pan or in the center of a 9 x 13 glass pan. Cover the top with a small piece of aluminum foil to prevent burning the top before the rest is completely cooked.

Bake at 350 degrees for about 1 hour and 20 minutes or until center is cooked through but still moist. Depending on oven, check at 1 hour. Let set for 5 minutes before slicing and serving.

coq au vin
italian style

Shared by Stage Neck Inn, York, Maine

	pinch salt	1	bunch thyme, chopped
	pinch pepper	1	bunch oregano, chopped
1/2	cup flour for tossing	1	bunch parsley, chopped
4	chicken legs/4 chicken thighs	2	tablespoons kosher salt
	canola oil, for searing chicken	1	tablespoon black pepper
1	onion, chopped	2	bay leaves
1	carrot, chopped	1	tablespoon paprika
2	ribs celery, chopped	1	large can whole peeled San Marzano tomatoes
1	garlic bulb, chopped	1	bottle Cabernet or Chianti wine
1	russet potato, chopped	2	cans chicken stock
1	bunch rosemary, chopped		

INSTRUCTIONS:

Mix salt, pepper and flour. Toss with chicken. On medium to high heat sear chicken, skin side down, in canola oil until brown on both sides. Remove from the pan.

Add all vegetables and herbs; brown slightly. Add tomatoes. Bring to a boil, lower heat. Add chicken, wine and stock. Simmer. Cover and place in oven at 250 degrees for 3 hours. For best results, cool finished dish, remove chicken and set aside. Reduce sauce by half and pour over chicken.

black watch farm meatloaf

Shared by Frank Manafort, Springfield, Vermont

1/2	cup milk	1/2	cup green pepper, chopped
1	egg, slightly beaten		
1 1/2	teaspoons chili powder	1/2	cup onion, chopped
1	teaspoon salt	1	tablespoon Tabasco sauce
1/2	teaspoon Italian seasoning		
	ground pepper, to taste	2	tablespoons Vermont maple syrup
1 1/2	cups bread crumbs	6	tablespoons ketchup
1 1/2	pounds Black Watch Farm ground beef*		brown sugar, to taste

INSTRUCTIONS:

In mixing bowl, combine milk, egg, seasonings, and bread crumbs. Let stand for about 5 minutes. Stir in ground beef, green peppers and onions; mix lightly but thoroughly. Shape meat mixture into loaf. Place in 13 x 9 x 2 baking dish. Bake in moderate oven at 350 degrees for 1 hour. Combine Tabasco sauce, maple syrup, ketchup and brown sugar; brush on meat loaf after 1 hour and return to the oven for approximately 10 minutes.

*See reference page 307

chicken florentine

Shared by Anita Gorman, Old Saybrook, Connecticut

4   boneless, skinless chicken breasts, halved

1   package frozen chopped spinach, thawed and drained

¹/₃ pound feta cheese

1   egg, beaten

1   can cream of chicken soup

¹/₃ cup milk

¹/₄ teaspoon dill

¹/₄ teaspoon oregano

¹/₄ teaspoon garlic, minced

salt, to taste

pepper, to taste

plain bread crumbs

INSTRUCTIONS:

Pound chicken halves to about ¹/₄ inch thickness. Combine spinach, feta cheese and egg in mixing bowl. Place a clump of mixture at end of chicken and roll. Place in baking dish. In separate bowl, combine chicken soup with milk until smooth. Add dill, oregano, garlic, salt and pepper; mix well. Pour mixture over chicken and sprinkle each piece of chicken with bread crumbs. Bake at 350 degrees for 45 minutes. Serve over a bed of rice or noodles. Serves 4.

perlow southern style

Shared by Diane Gardner, Madison, Connecticut

This is my version of my uncle Jack's recipe from Charleston, South Carolina. He cooks this outside in a big black iron pot over a fire! It is the most delicious comfort food. It takes a little time to prepare but is well worth the effort.

1	large chicken	1	large onion, chopped
4–5	cups broth from chicken	1	pound breakfast sausage, fried and chopped
2	cups rice, adjusted to the amount of broth		salt, to taste
1	pound bacon, fried and chopped		pepper, to taste

INSTRUCTIONS:

Fill a large pot with water and add chicken. Boil until tender. Remove chicken and debone. Measure the amount of broth. Use 2 cups broth for every cup of rice. Additional canned broth can be used if needed.

Set aside chicken, broth and measured rice. In the same large pot, fry bacon until crispy, chop and set aside. Add chopped onions to drippings of bacon and sauté. In another fry pan, cook sausage and chop into bite size pieces. Set aside.

When onions are soft, add the chicken and broth to the pot and bring to a simmer. Add rice, cover and let rice cook. Stir occasionally and when rice is almost done, add the sausage and bacon. Season with salt and pepper. If the rice mixture is too dry, add a little extra broth to keep moist. When rice is done, turn off and let sit to absorb all the flavors!

beef stew provençal

*Shared by Wesley Babb, LA Burdick's Post Office Café,
Walpole, New Hampshire*

*This dish has been in the restaurant since its beginning.
The dish is hearty, thick and delicious. The regional
assignment was coined for the tomatoes and olives used.
This is one of Burdick's signature dishes.*

2 pounds stew meat, veal or beef	1 large can whole plum tomatoes, strained, and crushed
1/2 bottle good red wine	3-4 cups veal or beef stock
salt, to taste	4–5 carrots, cut in 1/2 inch pieces
pepper, to taste	
olive oil, for coating pan	2 cloves garlic, whole
2 large onions, sliced thin	2 bay leaves, whole
1/4 cup orange juice	1/4 cup Kalamata olives

INSTRUCTIONS:

Day 1: Cover the stew meat with red wine and refrigerate for 24 hours.

Day 2: Preheat oven to 425 degrees.

Pour stew meat into a strainer, catching all wine in another dish. Let the meat strain for about 15 minutes. Once the meat is finished straining, place it onto a cookie sheet, single layer, and season with salt and pepper.

Place a roasting pan on moderate heat, getting it fairly hot. Then add enough oil to coat the bottom of pan. Add meat and sear well on all sides. Remove and set aside.

Place onions in pan and sauté until tender. Add wine and orange juice and reduce to almost nothing. Add tomatoes and stock to roasting pan. Bring to a simmer; add meat, making sure all is covered with stock. Add carrots, put garlic and bay leaves in sachet and add to pan. Cover with foil and place into oven for 1 hour. Then reduce temperature to 325 degrees and cook for 3 hours or until meat is tender. Reduce the stew until it thickens. Add the Kalamata olives before serving and top with whipped potato.

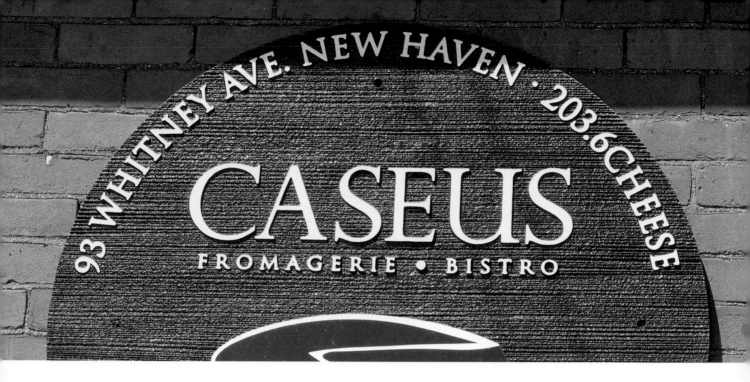

lamb leg steak
with dandelion mashed potatoes and sheep milk feta cilantro oil

Shared by Jason Sobocinski, Caseus Fromagerie Bistro, New Haven, Connecticut

4	large Idaho potatoes, peeled	4	butcher cut lamb leg steaks	
2	bunches dandelion greens, cut into 1-inch pieces		dried organic lavender	
2	tablespoons butter	1	bunch cilantro, chopped	
2	tablespoons plus 1 cup olive oil	1	small red onion, finely chopped	
	salt, to taste	4	ounce sheep milk feta cheese*, crumbled	
	pepper, to taste			

INSTRUCTIONS:

Place potatoes in a sauce pot with water. Boil until soft. Drain. Blanch dandelions in boiling water for 1 minute. Remove and place in ice water until cooled. Drain. Mash the potatoes with the butter and 2 tablespoons of oil. Season with salt and pepper. Add in dandelions and stir to combine. Grill lamb leg steaks over hot grill. Time will depend on thickness. Be sure to not overcook (they will continue to cook once off the grill). Place potatoes on a plate next to the steak; spoon cilantro oil over the meat. Combine the cilantro, red onion, and feta. Cover with the cup of olive oil. Season with salt, pepper and lavender.

*See reference page 307

mom's pot roast

Shared by Betsy Rudden, Farmington, Connecticut

My mom, Fran Rudden, made this pot roast every week. It was my favorite meal and it filled the house with the most delicious aroma. I still love to serve this meal.

flour, for browning roast

3 tablespoons Old Bay seasoning

1 4-pound bottom round roast

good olive oil

1 jelly glass of water (about 1 cup)

1/2 jelly glass of apple cider vinegar (about 1/2 cup)

1 large white onion, peeled and quartered

10 whole cloves

1 tablespoon salt

1 1/2 tablespoons pepper

1 pound carrots, peeled

INSTRUCTIONS:

Mix the flour and Old Bay seasoning together. Roll the roast on all sides to cover with flour mixture. Cover the bottom of a heavy stock pot, with olive oil and heat to medium. Brown the roast on all sides until a light brown crust forms.

Place the browned meat with the water and vinegar into a crock pot. Add the onion, cloves, salt and pepper. Cover and cook on high for 1 hour. Reduce the temperature to low and continue cooking until a fork inserts easily into the center of the meat, usually 6–7 hours. Approximately 1 hour before serving, add the peeled carrots and cook through. When the carrots are cooked, remove the meat and carrots and place on platter. Cover with foil.

Turn the crock pot up to high and bring to a liquid boil. To make the gravy; thoroughly incorporate all the ingredients using a stick blender. Depending on the consistency of the sauce, add flour in tablespoon increments to reach desired consistency. Taste the gravy and season with salt and pepper if needed.

Slice the meat, which by now will just about fall apart, and serve with chunky mashed potatoes, the cooked carrots and lots of the delicious gravy.

Variation: While not part of Mom's original recipe, try adding ten Moravian ginger snap cookies at the end and blend these into the gravy. It really adds interesting flavor and makes the taste even more intense.

simon's meatloaf

Shared by Simon's Marketplace, Chester, Connecticut

1 medium onion, chopped

1 clove garlic, chopped
   olive oil, for sautéing

2½ pounds ground beef

2 eggs

½ cup heavy cream

2 teaspoons dried oregano

1 teaspoon salt

½ cup Asian sweet chili sauce

2 cups Panko bread crumbs

1½ teaspoons coarse sea salt

INSTRUCTIONS:

Sauté onion and garlic in olive oil. In a mixing bowl, add ground beef, eggs, heavy cream, oregano, salt, sautéed onion and garlic and sweet chili sauce. Mix until well blended. Add bread crumbs and mix again. Form into a loaf on a sheet tray or baking dish. Coat the meatloaf with sweet chili sauce to form a glaze. Sprinkle the top with coarse sea salt. Bake at 350 degrees for about 45 minutes to 1 hour. Remove from oven and let rest for about ½ hour before slicing. This will keep the meatloaf moist.

desserts

tiramisu

cranberry apple crumb pie

coconut cream pie

frozen blackberry marshmallow pie

rudden's mud pie

scandinavian almond cake

betty's damn good cookies

rice pudding

crunchy peanut butter balls

potato chip cookies

red velvet cake

gingerbread white chocolate
chunk cookies

apple dapple cake

lemon sponge pie

granny's sweet cream pound cake
with caramel frosting

chocolate mousse

desserts

christmas yule log

pumpkin cookies with cream
cheese frosting

date bars with oatmeal

chocolate cake

vermont maple walnut pie

chocolate brownie

frozen key lime pie

ruth's berry cobbler

butternut squash pie

alaskan raspberry blueberry
coffeecake

joan's incredible edibles

southern pecan pie

lemon filled coconut cake

ricotta pie

pineapple cheese pie

desserts

scandinavian almond cookies

bread pudding "by guess or gory"

claire's country garden mincemeat
drop cookies

flaky, tasty pie crust mix

chocolate banana bread

dark chocolate brownies

swedish creme

mother's lemon sherbet

di's blueberry pie

maple glazed poached pears

shortcake biscuits

fresh apple pound cake

chocolate applesauce cake

pumpkin pie cake

lemon yogurt cake

tiramisu

Shared by Sardella's Restaurant, Newport, Rhode Island

*Sardella's has been in business for more than
28 years and has been visited by many famous people,
all of whom love our famous tiramisu! This is a must have
when visiting Newport. And it's also a favorite of the locals
who dine with us all year long.*

24 ladyfingers, split lengthwise	14 ounces mascarpone cheese
³/4 cup espresso coffee, cooled	2 tablespoons amaretto, brandy or Kahlua
6 eggs, separated	8 ounces bittersweet chocolate, chopped or coarsely grated
6 tablespoons sugar	

INSTRUCTIONS:

Heat oven to 375 degrees. Arrange ladyfingers on a baking sheet and bake until toasted golden, 5–10 minutes.

Arrange half the ladyfingers in a 2 or 2¹/₂-inch deep oval or rectangular serving dish. Brush lightly with espresso.

In a large mixing bowl, beat egg whites at high speed with electric mixer until they are stiff. Set aside. In a small mixing bowl, beat egg yolks and sugar at medium speed with electric mixer until thick and lemon colored. Add mascarpone cheese and amaretto. Stir gently. Gently fold egg whites into the mascarpone mixture. Spread half the mixture on the ladyfingers in the serving dish, then sprinkle with half the chocolate. Repeat layers of ladyfingers, mascarpone mixture and chocolate. Keep refrigerated. Serves 6.

cranberry apple crumb pie

Shared by Marie Walston, Guilford, Connecticut
This is a must have on Thanksgiving!

PIE:

5–6	cups apples, sliced (like Empires)
	freshly squeezed lemon juice
1–1¹/₂	cups fresh cranberries
¹/₄	cup all purpose flour
1	cup sugar
1	teaspoon cinnamon
1	unbaked pie crust

CRUMB TOPPING:

1	cup all purpose flour
¹/₂	cup sugar
1	teaspoon cinnamon
¹/₂	cup unsalted butter, softened

INSTRUCTIONS:

Preheat oven to 400 degrees. Put apples into large bowl and squeeze with lemon juice to keep from browning. Add cranberries and toss. Combine flour, sugar and cinnamon and pour over fruit mixture to cover. Pour fruit mixture into pie crust. Make the crumb topping by combining flour, sugar and cinnamon in bowl. Use hands to combine the softened butter with the dry mixture. Sprinkle crumb topping evenly over the filled crust.

Bake for 45–50 minutes until golden brown. Wait until the steaming pink juice from the cranberries oozes out through the crumb; that is when the pie is done.

coconut cream pie

Shared by Loretta Tallevast, Lake City, South Carolina

This is another must have Southern delight! My mama, Sybil Anderson, always used to make coconut pies and coconut cakes. At every family get together, whether it was Sunday afternoon dinner or Thanksgiving, you could count on having coconut cream pie.

PIE:

2	large eggs yolks
1	pint milk
1	cup sugar
2	tablespoons cornstarch
	pinch salt
1	tablespoon butter

1/2	teaspoon vanilla
1	cup fresh coconut or 6-ounce pack frozen, shredded
1	8-inch pie shell, baked

MERINGUE:

2	egg whites
1/4	cup sugar

1/4	teaspoon cream of tartar

INSTRUCTIONS:

Beat yolks into ³/₄ cup of milk. Heat in heavy saucepan. Mix sugar, cornstarch, salt and remaining milk. Blend with the first mixture. Add butter. Stir until mixture thickens and sticks to the spoon.

Remove from the stove and add vanilla and coconut to the cream filling. Pour into pie shell.

For meringue, beat egg whites until stiff. Add sugar and cream of tartar. Spread on top of pie and bake at 350 degrees until brown.

frozen blackberry marshmallow pie

Shared by a local from Jonesboro, Maine

CRUST:

¹/₂ cup flour	¹/₄ cup butter, softened
¹/₄ cup brown sugar	¹/₃ cup pecans, chopped

FILLING:

¹/₄ cup lemon juice	3 cups blackberries
1 cup marshmallow creme	1 cup heavy cream

INSTRUCTIONS:

Preheat oven to 350 degrees. Combine flour and sugar for crust. Cut in butter and add nuts. Press into 8-inch springform pan. Bake 20 minutes at 350 degrees. Cool.

Gradually mix lemon juice with marshmallow creme. Stir in blackberries. Whip heavy cream and fold into blackberry mixture. Pour into crust lined pan and freeze for 4 hours. Serves 8–12.

rudden's mud pie

Shared by Dyana Rudden, Branford, Connecticut

¹/₂-³/₄ package chocolate wafers	1¹/₂-2 cups fudge sauce
¹/₂ stick butter, melted	whipped cream, to taste
1 gallon coffee (or any flavor) ice cream, softened	shaved chocolate, for garnish
	almonds, to taste

INSTRUCTIONS:

Crush wafers and pour into pie plate. Add melted butter and press to form crust. Cover with softened ice cream. Top with fudge sauce. If fudge is very cold, it will spread easier. Place the pie in the freezer overnight. When ready to serve, top with whipped cream and shaved chocolate or sliced almonds.

scandinavian almond cake

Shared by Marcia Carlson, East Orleans, Massachusetts

$1/4$–$1/2$ cup almonds, sliced

$1^1/4$ cups sugar

1 egg

$1^1/2$ teaspoons pure almond extract

$2/3$ cup milk

$1^1/4$ cups flour

$1/2$ teaspoon baking powder

1 stick butter, melted

confectioners' sugar, for sprinkling top

INSTRUCTIONS:

Preheat oven to 350 degrees. Spray 13 x 9 pan with Pam and sprinkle sliced almonds on the bottom. Beat the sugar, egg, almond extract and milk together. Add the flour and baking powder, mix and then add the butter. Mix well. Bake at 350 degrees for 40–50 minutes, until the edges are golden brown. Cool in pan before removing and sprinkle with confectioners' sugar. Cake will break if removed too soon.

betty's damn good cookies

Shared by Judy Brawn, Dexter, Maine

Betty lived up the road from us on a farm. When asked what the name of her cookie was, she said, "Betty's Damn Good Cookies"! This will become one of your favorite cookie recipes, too.

1	cup white sugar	1	teaspoon soda
1	cup brown sugar	1	teaspoon salt
1	cup Crisco shortening	2	cups old fashioned oatmeal
1	cup peanut butter		
3	eggs	2	teaspoons vanilla
1½	cups flour	1	12-ounce bag chocolate bits

INSTRUCTIONS:

Combine all ingredients and bake at 375 degrees for about 10–12 minutes. These are good pulled when still a little soft.

rice pudding

Shared by Carol Kenyhercz, Branford, Connecticut

¾	cup long grain rice	¾	cup sugar
6	cups milk	2	teaspoons vanilla
3	egg yolks		sprinkle cinnamon
1	cup heavy cream		

INSTRUCTIONS:

Put rice and milk into a saucepan and bring to a boil, then lower immediately. Stir occasionally; there should always be "little bubbles" in the pot while cooking. Do this for 55 minutes, until rice is absorbed but not too thick.

Put egg yolks in a bowl and beat thoroughly. Add heavy cream and blend, then add sugar and vanilla. When rice and milk are cooked, stir in the egg mixture. Boil until sugar is completely blended. Pour into an oblong dish, cool completely on a wire rack, then refrigerate. Just before serving, sprinkle cinnamon on top. Add raisins or any type of candied fruit if desired.

crunchy peanut butter balls

Shared by Viola Faulkingham, Addison, Maine

A simple recipe I make to give to my friends when they stop by for a visit. I like to pack a few to send home with them as a little surprise.

1	cup smooth peanut butter	1½ cups semisweet chocolate chips
1	7-ounce jar marshmallow creme	4 teaspoons shortening
1½ cups Rice Krispies		

INSTRUCTIONS:

Combine peanut butter, marshmallow creme and Rice Krispies in a bowl. Roll teaspoons of mix into 1-inch balls.

Melt chocolate chips with shortening in a double boiler. Dip balls into the melted chocolate. Place onto wax paper and refrigerate.

potato chip cookies

Shared by Helen Winokur, Madison, Connecticut

1	cup margarine	¹/₂	cup potato chips, finely crushed
¹/₂	cup sugar		
1	egg yolk	¹/₂	cup pecans, chopped
1	teaspoon vanilla	1	box confectioners' sugar, enough for rolling cookies
1¹/₂	cups flour		

INSTRUCTIONS:

Cream the margarine and sugar. Add the egg yolk, vanilla and flour. Crush the potato chips, using a food processor. Stir chips and nuts into batter. Drop by teaspoonful or cookie scoop onto an ungreased cookie sheet. Use a silpat for this.

Bake for 15 minutes in a preheated oven at 350 degrees. Cool slightly and roll in confectioners' sugar.

red velvet cake

Shared by Diane Gardner, Madison, Connecticut
This is a cake I grew up with. To me,
this is a true Southern delight.

CAKE:

1/2 cup Crisco shortening	1 teaspoon almond flavoring
1 1/2 cups sugar	1 teaspoon vanilla
2 eggs	1 cup buttermilk
1 2-ounce bottle red food coloring	2 1/4 cups plain flour
3 tablespoons cocoa	1 1/2 teaspoons baking soda
1/2 teaspoon salt	1 tablespoon cider vinegar

INSTRUCTIONS:

Cream Crisco and sugar well. Add eggs, 1 at a time, and beat after each one. Make paste of food coloring and cocoa; add this to sugar mixture.

Mix salt, almond flavoring, vanilla and buttermilk. Alternately add the flour and then the buttermilk mixture to the sugar mixture until all is combined. Mix soda and vinegar and fold into the batter.

Pour into 2 greased and floured cake pans. Bake at 350 degrees for 30 minutes or until toothpick comes clean. Cool in pan for 5 minutes and put on wire rack to cool completely.

When cooled, split cake layers in half to make 4 layers.

ICING:

2 sticks butter, softened	2 boxes powdered sugar
2 8-ounce packages cream cheese, softened	3 teaspoons vanilla

INSTRUCTIONS:

Cream butter and cream cheese until light and fluffy. Add sugar and vanilla. Beat slowly with electric mixer until of good spreading consistency. Spread between layers and sides of cake, using all the icing. Refrigerate. It is best to cool cake and refrigerate for 1 or 2 days before serving. Remove from refrigerator 30 minutes before serving.

gingerbread white chocolate chunk cookies

Shared by Kate Walston, Guilford, Connecticut

This cookie was inspired by the autumnal flavor of warm gingerbread with whipped cream, a popular item on many Maine dessert menus.

1 teaspoon baking soda	1½ cups flour
1½ teaspoons hot water	1 teaspoon cinnamon
1 stick unsalted butter, room temperature	1¼ teaspoons ground ginger
½ cup light brown sugar, packed	⅛ teaspoon ground cloves
¼ cup honey	7 ounces white chocolate, chopped into chunks
¼ cup molasses	⅓ cup granulated sugar

INSTRUCTIONS:

Preheat oven to 325 degrees. Line 2 baking sheets with parchment paper or grease.

Dissolve baking soda in hot water. With a mixer, cream together butter and brown sugar. Add honey and molasses; beat until combined.

Sift together remaining dry ingredients (except for granulated sugar). Beat half of the flour mixture into the butter mixture, then beat in baking soda mixture, then beat in remaining flour until combined. Mix in white chocolate. Wrap dough in plastic wrap and chill in the fridge until firm.

Roll dough into 1½-inch balls and roll each ball in the sugar. Place 2 inches apart on prepared baking sheets. Bake 12 minutes. Allow to cool on wire rack. Store airtight.

apple dapple cake

Shared by Fran Gardner, Florence, South Carolina

3	eggs	1	teaspoon baking soda
1	cup plus 1 tablespoon oil	2	teaspoons vanilla extract
2	cups sugar	3	cups apples, peeled and chopped
3	cups all purpose flour		
1	teaspoon salt	1½	cups pecans, chopped

SAUCE:

1	cup brown sugar	1	stick margarine
¼	cup milk		

INSTRUCTIONS:

Mix eggs, oil and sugar, blend well. Add flour, salt and baking soda and mix well. Add vanilla along with the apples and nuts. Mix and put into an 8 or 9-inch tube pan. Bake at 350 degrees for 1 hour.

To make sauce, combine sugar, milk and margarine and cook for 2½ minutes. Pour hot topping over hot cake. Do not remove the cake until it is COLD.

lemon sponge pie

Shared by Joan Hodge Joos, Hopkinton, New Hampshire
This is from our grandmother, Emily Curtis Tinker.
A great old-fashioned lemon sponge pie!

1 cup sugar	1 lemon, juice and grated rind
3 tablespoons flour	
2–3 egg yolks	1 cup milk
butter, size of a walnut, softened	2–3 egg whites, stiffly beaten
	1 unbaked pie crust

INSTRUCTIONS:

Beat sugar, flour, yolks and butter to a cream. Add lemon juice and grated rind. Gradually blend in milk. Fold in egg whites. Bake in pie crust at 450 degrees for 10 minutes, then at 325 degrees for 35 minutes. Delicious.

granny's sweet cream pound cake

with caramel frosting

Shared by Loretta Tallevast, Brenda Martin and JoEllen Odom, sisters, all living in South Carolina

We grew up playing outside to the smell of this famous Lake City pound cake cooling in the window sill. We knew we were in for a treat when the aroma of this hit the neighborhood! One call for dinner and we came running, eating as fast as possible in order to get to dessert. Now we make this cake, and we cut it right away; it doesn't even make it to dessert. We sometimes ice it with caramel frosting; now there's a special treat.

3   cups sugar

3   sticks butter, softened

6   eggs, room temperature

3   cups Swans Down cake flour, sifted

½   pint heavy whipping cream

1   teaspoon vanilla

INSTRUCTIONS:

Let sugar, butter and eggs reach room temperature. Leave them out overnight for baking the next day.

Combine sugar and butter until creamy. Add eggs, 1 at a time, and blend each time. Mix well. Alternately add 1 cup of flour followed by one third of the whipping cream, until all is added. Add vanilla at the end and mix well. Pour into a well-greased tube pan.

Do not preheat oven. Bake for 1½ hours at 300 degrees or until done.

caramel frosting

This is simply the best caramel frosting you will ever have.

1   box brown sugar

³/₄ cup Pet milk

1¹/₂ sticks butter

²/₃ cup confectioners' sugar

¹/₄ teaspoon baking powder

INSTRUCTIONS:

Mix first 4 ingredients together and bring to a boil on stove, medium heat, for 4 minutes. Remove from stove and add baking powder. Let stand for 5 minutes. Whip with mixer for about 10–15 minutes. Ice cake, using all the frosting.

chocolate mousse

Shared by Carol Kenyhercz, Branford, Connecticut
*This mousse is best when made a day or two ahead
and refrigerated.*

8	eggs	¼ cup flavored brandy,
1	large package semisweet chocolate bits	optional
		fresh whipped cream,
10	tablespoons unsalted butter	for serving

INSTRUCTIONS:

Separate eggs, putting whites into a large bowl and yolks into a small
bowl. Let egg whites warm to room temperature–1 hour. In top of a
double boiler, over hot but not boiling water, melt semisweet chocolate
with butter, stirring constantly.

Remove top of double boiler from water. Using a wooden spoon, beat egg
yolks, 1 at a time, beating well after each addition. It's best to beat the
egg yolks separately, then add to the chocolate. Let cool for 10 minutes,
then add brandy.

With mixer, beat egg whites until stiff; moist peaks form when the
beater is slowly raised. With a wire whisk or rubber scraper, using an
under and over motion, gently fold chocolate mixture into egg whites,
just enough to combine thoroughly; there should be no white streaks.

Pour into an attractive service dish or use individual serving glasses.
Cover with Saran wrap and refrigerate. When serving, decorate with
fresh whipped cream.

christmas yule log

Shared by Joan Hodge Joos, Hopkinton, New Hampshire

CAKE:

6   egg whites

³/₄ cup sugar

6   egg yolks

¹/₃ cup unsweetened cocoa

1¹/₂ teaspoons vanilla

FILLING:

1¹/₂ cups heavy cream,
     whipped

¹/₂ cup confectioners' sugar

¹/₄ cup cocoa

2   teaspoons instant coffee
     vanilla, to taste

INSTRUCTIONS:

Grease and line a jelly roll pan with waxed paper. Beat egg whites until stiff with ¹/₄ cup sugar. With same beaters, beat yolks with rest of sugar until thick. Add cocoa and vanilla and fold in beaten egg whites.

Bake at 375 degrees for 15 minutes.

Combine filling ingredients together and set aside.

Turn pan over onto dish towel; roll with towel, jelly roll fashion. Cool. Gently unroll, spread with filling and reroll. Sprinkle with confectioners' sugar. Refrigerate.

pumpkin cookies
with cream cheese frosting

Shared by Robin Walston, Stratham, New Hampshire

2¹/₂ cups flour	¹/₂ cup butter, softened
1 teaspoon baking soda	1¹/₂ cups sugar
1 teaspoon baking powder	1 cup canned pumpkin
1 teaspoon ground cinnamon	1 egg
¹/₂ teaspoon nutmeg	1 teaspoon vanilla
¹/₂ teaspoon salt	1 can cream cheese frosting

INSTRUCTIONS:

Preheat oven to 375 degrees. Combine flour, baking soda, baking powder, cinnamon, nutmeg and salt in medium bowl. Cream butter and sugar in larger bowl. Add pumpkin, egg and vanilla; beat until light and creamy. Mix in dry ingredients until well blended. Drop by rounded tablespoons onto a greased cookie sheet. Bake for 18–20 minutes or until done. Let cool. Top with cream cheese frosting.

date bars
with oatmeal

Shared by Susie Birk, Madison, Connecticut
This recipe comes from my grandmother, Emily Curtis Tinker.

1	package dates	1 ½	cups flour
½	cup sugar	1	cup brown sugar
1	lemon, juiced	¾	cup butter or Crisco
	dash salt		(or ½ of each)
1 ½	cups Quick Quaker oats	½	teaspoon baking soda

INSTRUCTIONS:

Dice dates and cook with just enough water to cover until tender; about 10 minutes. Add sugar and continue to cook until liquid is clear. Add lemon juice and salt and let cool.

Mix oats, flour and brown sugar with butter, then add baking soda. Blend until evenly mixed. Press slightly more than half of this mixture into a greased 9-inch square pan. Add date mixture and the remaining crumbs on top.

Pat lightly and bake at 375 degrees for 25 minutes. Cut into squares.

chocolate cake

Shared by Agnes Wright, Lake City, South Carolina

This is the best 10 or 12-layer chocolate cake you will ever make. It is made the old-fashioned way with cooked icing and very thin layers.

CAKE:

2   sticks butter, room temperature

½   cup sugar

5   eggs, room temperature

1   teaspoon vanilla

1   cup self-rising flour

1   box Duncan Hines butter cake mix

1   large can evaporated milk

INSTRUCTIONS:

Cream butter and sugar; add eggs 1 at a time. Add remaining ingredients and mix well. Bake layers at 350 degrees for 18 minutes. You can get 5 or 6 thick layers from this batch. Let cake cool and use plain dental floss to cut each layer in half, making 10 or 12 very thin layers.

FROSTING:

½–¾ cup cocoa, sifted

3½   cups sugar

2   large cans evaporated milk

¾   stick butter or margarine

2   teaspoons vanilla

INSTRUCTIONS:

Sift cocoa into sugar. Mix well, then add evaporated milk. Cook on medium heat until mixture begins to boil. Add butter and vanilla. Stir with wooden spoon. Mixture will begin to thicken; continue to cook until mixture coats wooden spoon well. This takes approximately 45 minutes. Stir chocolate mixture well before removing from heat. Do not stir again. Spread on layers while frosting is hot.

vermont maple walnut pie

*Shared by Paradise Farm Sugarhouse,
West Brattleboro, Vermont*

3	eggs	4	tablespoons unsalted butter, melted
⅓	cup sugar		
¼	teaspoon salt	1	cup walnut pieces
1	cup pure Vermont maple syrup	1	unbaked pie shell

INSTRUCTIONS:

Heat oven to 375 degrees. Add eggs, sugar, salt and syrup to a bowl. While mixing, add melted butter. Pour walnuts into pie shell, then add the liquid mixture. Bake 30–40 minutes. Let pie cool to room temperature before serving.

chocolate brownies

Shared by Rick Crean, Chatham Bakery,
Chatham, Massachusetts

4	ounces bittersweet chocolate	1³/₄	cups sugar
1	cup butter	1¹/₂	teaspoons vanilla extract
2	large or 3 small eggs	1¹/₄	cups cake flour, sifted

INSTRUCTIONS:

Over double broiler, melt the chocolate and butter; set aside. Mix the eggs, sugar and vanilla; beat lightly. Add melted chocolate and mix. Add sifted flour and mix until incorporated. Bake at 350 degrees for about 30 minutes or until toothpick comes out clean. Add a layer of favorite white frosting and put in freezer until icing hardens. Then remove and add a layer of chocolate frosting.

frozen key lime pie

Shared by Marie Waltson, Guilford, Connecticut
On the birthdays of my husband and kids, I make their
favorite cake or pie. My daughter-in-law Abbie often
picks key lime pie. Her other favorite is ice cream.
So I made up this recipe to combine her favorites. Enjoy!

CRUST:

³/₄–1	**cup flour**
¹/₂	**cup brown sugar**
¹/₂	**cup butter, softened**
²/₃	**cup pecans, finely chopped**

INSTRUCTIONS:

Preheat oven to 350 degrees. Combine flour and sugar. Cut in butter and add nuts. Press in 9-inch springform pan. Bake 20 minutes at 350 degrees. Cool completely.

FILLING:

6	**egg yolks**
1	**can sweetened condensed milk**
1	**full cup vanilla ice cream, softened**
¹/₂	**cup "real" key lime juice**
1	**cup heavy cream, whipped lime wedges, for garnish**

INSTRUCTIONS:

Combine egg yolks and condensed milk and beat on high speed until thick and fluffy. Add the ice cream and blend completely on lowest speed of mixer. Add key lime juice and blend well. Fold in the whipped cream until combined and smooth. Pour into cool pie shell. Place in freezer until well set, at least 4–5 hours. Garnish with whipped cream and lime wedges.

ruth's berry cobbler

Ruth Carver, Beals Island, Maine

Working at Senior high church camp in July at Camp Winniaugwamauk in Brooksville, we make enough cobbler to feed 60 to 70 campers every summer.

	raspberries, strawberries, blueberries	1/2	cup unsalted butter, softened
	sprinkle cinnamon	3	cups sugar
	lemon juice	1	cup milk
2	cups flour	2	heaping teaspoons cornstarch
2	teaspoons baking powder	1 1/2	cups boiling water
	pinch salt		whipped cream, for garnish

INSTRUCTIONS:

Preheat oven to 350 degrees. Grease a 9 x 13 pan. Fill pan half full with mixed berries. Sprinkle berries with cinnamon. Dribble with lemon juice.

Combine flour, baking powder and salt. Set aside in bowl. Cream together butter and 1 1/2 cups sugar. Combine flour mixture with butter mixture alternating with milk. Pour cake batter evenly on top of all the berries and set aside.

Mix 1 1/2 cups of sugar with cornstarch, and sprinkle evenly over batter. Pour 1 1/2 cups of boiling water all over the top of the cake (yes, right over the sugar and cornstarch). Bake for 1 hour. Let cool and serve with a dollop of whipped cream.

butternut squash pie

Shared by Abigail Rose Walston, Guilford, Connecticut

My great grandma Marion Rose always made her pumpkin pie with butternut squash, saying it made a better pie. I've been making this version for years and just won Best in Show at the Guilford Fair.

1	cup squash puree	1	teaspoon cinnamon
1	cup heavy cream	1	teaspoon nutmeg
1	cup sugar	½	teaspoon salt
3	eggs, beaten		pie dough for
2	tablespoons water		9 or 10-inch crust

INSTRUCTIONS:

To make puree, split 1 butternut squash lengthwise, scoop out the seeds and remove the stem. Place squash cut side down on a baking pan and bake at 375 degrees for about 1 hour, until soft. Allow to cool and then scoop pulp into a food processor and puree.

Preheat oven to 425 degrees. Line a pie pan with the dough and crimp the edges. Combine all ingredients in a large bowl and whisk until smooth. Pour into pie crust and bake for 10 minutes. Reduce heat to 300 degrees and bake for 50–60 more minutes, until the filling is slightly puffed and the bottom crust is golden brown. Use a glass baking dish so the crust can be monitored; and if it's not browning nicely, put it on the bottom rack of the oven for 10 minutes. Let the pie cool completely so the filling will set before cutting it. It tastes even better the second day, when it's cold from the refrigerator.

alaskan raspberry blueberry coffeecake

Shared by Kim Kezer, Amesbury, Massachusetts

This a great recipe that was served to us at a bed and breakfast in Gustavus, Alaska, near Glacier Bay.

CAKE:

1/2 cup butter, room temperature	2 1/4 cups flour
1 cup sugar	1 teaspoon baking soda
3 eggs	2 teaspoons baking powder
1 cup milk	2 cups fresh or frozen blueberries
2 teaspoons vanilla	1 cup fresh red raspberries

TOPPING:

3/4 cup sugar	3 teaspoons fresh lemon juice

INSTRUCTIONS:

In large bowl, cream butter and sugar until fluffy. Add eggs, then milk and then vanilla. Beat until thoroughly blended. Mix in flour, baking soda and baking powder. Divide between two greased 9-inch round pans. Sprinkle berries over the batter in each pan. Mix topping and sprinkle over coffeecakes.

Bake at 350 degrees for 35–40 minutes or until wooden pick comes out clean. Serve warm with butter.

joan's incredible edibles

Shared by Louise Worrell, Killingworth, Connecticut

These treats are the best. If you love Reese's Peanut Butter Cups, you will love these. My family is chock full of incredible cooks and bakers. Unfortunately, I don't have their gift and don't even attempt to try. However, this is the one thing I can make that looks special, tastes yummy and is simple to make.

³/₄ cup butter or margarine, melted

2 cups confectioners' sugar

2 cups graham cracker crumbs

1 12-ounce jar smooth peanut butter

12 ounces semisweet chocolate chips

INSTRUCTIONS:

Mix the first 4 ingredients and press into a 9 x 13 pan. Then melt chocolate chips and spread over the peanut butter mixture. Refrigerate. Cut immediately after the chocolate hardens so there are no cracks in the chocolate. Makes 48 bars.

southern pecan pie

Shared by Loretta Tallevast, Lake City, South Carolina

If you travel down south, you will always find pecan pie on the menu. A Southern dinner is not complete without a good ole' Southern pecan pie. This pie will melt in your mouth. Fresh out of the oven with a scoop of vanilla ice cream, it doesn't get any better than that.

1	unbaked pie shell	½	cup dark Karo syrup
3	eggs, well beaten	¼	cup butter, melted
1	cup sugar	1	cup pecans, chopped

INSTRUCTIONS:

Prebake pie shell at 400 degrees for 3–5 minutes to keep crust from being soft.

Beat eggs; stir in sugar, syrup and melted butter. Fold in pecans. Pour into pie shell and bake for 35–40 minutes at 375 degrees. This is simple and so delicious. Enjoy!

lemon filled coconut cake

Shared by a local in Hartland, Vermont

CAKE:

1	cup butter, softened	3¼	teaspoons baking powder
2	cups superfine sugar	¾	teaspoon salt
3	eggs	1½	cups milk
3	teaspoons pure vanilla		
3¼	cups all purpose flour		

FILLING:

1	cup sugar	4	egg yolks
¼	cup cornstarch	⅓	cup lemon juice
1	cup water	2	tablespoons butter

FROSTING:

1½	cups sugar	¼	teaspoon cream of tartar
2	egg whites	2	teaspoons vanilla extract
⅓	cup water	2–3	cups coconut flakes

INSTRUCTIONS:

Cream butter and sugar until light and fluffy. Add eggs 1 at a time and blend well. Beat in vanilla. Combine flour, baking powder and salt then add to creamed mix, alternating with milk. Pour into 3 greased and floured pans; bake at 350 degrees for 25 minutes. Cool 10 minutes before turning onto wire rack.

For the filling, combine sugar, cornstarch and water until smooth. Bring to a boil; cook and stir for 2 minutes longer until thick and bubbly. Remove from heat. Stir a small amount of hot mix into egg yolks and return pan to heat, stirring constantly. Bring to a gentle boil. Cook 2 minutes longer, remove from heat and stir in lemon juice and butter. Cool to room temperature without stirring.

For the frosting, combine sugar, egg whites, water and cream of tartar in a heavy saucepan. With a hand mixer, beat on low speed for 1 minute. Continue to beat on low speed until temperature reaches 160 degrees, about 10 minutes. Transfer to a large bowl and add vanilla. Beat on high until stiff peaks form, about 7 minutes.

Place 1 layer on cake plate, spread with half of the filling and repeat. Frost top and sides of cake, sprinkle with coconut and store in refrigerator.

ricotta pie

Shared by Mary Dangelo, Narragansett, Rhode Island

The day before Easter I make a couple of these ricotta pies, one to bring to the family dinner and one to leave at home. They get better as each day passes. This comes from a small book called The Home Book of Italian Cooking that I have had my 60 years of married life.

1½ pounds ricotta cheese

¾ cup sugar

¼ cup flour

2 tablespoons lemon juice

3 eggs, separated

½ pint heavy cream

2 unbaked 9-inch pie shells (I like a pie crust that is sweetened with a bit of sugar)

powdered sugar, for dusting

INSTRUCTIONS:

Mix ricotta with sugar, then blend in the flour and lemon juice. Beat thoroughly. Beat egg yolks until thick and lemon colored and fold them into the ricotta. Beat cream until stiff and fold gently into the ricotta mixture. Beat egg whites until stiff and fold into the ricotta mixture. Pour filling into unbaked pie shells and bake in slow 300 degree oven for 1 hour. Pies will be just set. Turn off oven heat and leave the pies in the oven without opening the door for 1 hour.

Remove from oven and cool thoroughly. Dust tops with powdered sugar. Serves 12.

pineapple cheese pie

Shared by Anita Gorman, Old Saybrook, Connecticut

CRUST:

1³/₄ cups graham cracker crumbs

¹/₄ cup sugar

¹/₂ cup butter, softened

FILLING:

1 12-ounce package cream cheese, softened

¹/₂ teaspoon vanilla extract

¹/₂ cup sugar

¹/₈ teaspoon cinnamon

2 eggs, slightly beaten

1 can crushed pineapple, well drained

TOPPING:

1 cup sour cream

3 tablespoons sugar

1 teaspoon vanilla

INSTRUCTIONS:

Mix together the crumbs and sugar. Using a fork, blend in butter. Press mixture in a 9-inch deep dish pie plate. Bake at 375 degrees for 5 minutes. Let cool.

For the pie filling, blend together, using a mixer, the cream cheese and vanilla. Blending until smooth, add gradually the sugar, cinnamon and eggs. Gently blend in drained pineapple. Turn into crust. Bake at 325 degrees for about 35–40 minutes, until top feels set when touched.

Mix together ingredients for the topping, while pie is baking. When pie is done, remove from the oven and spread topping over hot pie. Topping will set as pie cools. When cooled, refrigerate thoroughly before serving.

scandinavian almond cookies

Shared by Kate Walston, Guilford, Connecticut

At Christmas time my mom and I always bake hundreds of cookies. We make beautiful Italian cookie trays but also include our friends' and family's special American favorites. Over time the tray has defined itself with staples, making little room for something new to try every year. A longtime favorite, and still standing, are these almond cookies that can be enjoyed any time of year.

COOKIES:

1¾ cups flour

2 teaspoons baking powder

¼ teaspoon salt

½ cup unsalted butter, room temperature

1 cup sugar

1 egg

½ teaspoon almond extract

½ cup almonds, sliced, lightly toasted or raw

INSTRUCTIONS:

Preheat oven to 325 degrees.

Sift together flour, baking powder, salt. With a mixer, cream together butter and sugar till fluffy. Add egg and almond extract and beat well. Add flour mixture and beat until well mixed.

Divide dough into 3 equal parts. Form each into a 12-inch log, then place 2 logs 4 to 5 inches apart on an ungreased cookie sheet, and the last log on another cookie sheet. Flatten each log until 3½ inches wide.

Bake at 325 degrees for 12–14 minutes or until edges are lightly browned. While cookies are still warm, cut them crosswise at a diagonal into 1-inch wide strips. Transfer to a wire rack to cool.

ALMOND ICING:

1 cup powdered sugar

¼ teaspoon almond extract

3–4 teaspoons milk

INSTRUCTIONS:

Whisk together all ingredients to create a smooth drizzly consistency.

Drizzle icing over bars and sprinkle with almonds immediately. Allow to dry. Store airtight.

bread pudding
"by guess or by gory"

Shared by Lita Lynfesty Beal, Beals Island, Maine

I call this "by guess or by gory" because these old recipes
that have been passed down from generation to generation
are not very detailed. It is a tad of this and a pinch
of that or, as we say on the Island, by guess or by gory.
You have to read between the lines! Good recipe for
a crowd, church suppers and church camps.

1	loaf stale bread, broken into small pieces	$^1/_4$	teaspoon salt
3–4	eggs	1	stick unsalted butter, melted
$^1/_4$–$^1/_2$	cup sugar		cinnamon, optional
2	cups milk, scalded		apple pieces, optional
$^1/_2$–1	teaspoon vanilla		butter, for dotting top

INSTRUCTIONS:

Combine all ingredients except the bread. Butter a large baking pan.
Place the bread pieces in a large bowl and pour the custard mixture over
the bread. It is optional, but you can add a large dash of cinnamon or
apple pieces if desired. Be sure the bread sets a few minutes as to get
very moist with the egg mixture. Pour into baking pan, dot with butter
and bake for 1 hour on 350 degrees.

claire's mincemeat drop cookies

Shared by Claire's Country Garden, Alburgh, Vermont

3¼ cups flour, sifted	1 teaspoon vanilla
½ teaspoon salt	1 cup sugar
1 teaspoon baking soda	3 eggs, unbeaten
1 teaspoon cinnamon	1½ cups mincemeat*
½ cup shortening	1 cup raisins
1 cup butter, softened	1 cup nuts, chopped

INSTRUCTIONS:

Sift together flour, salt, baking soda and cinnamon; set aside. Combine shortening, butter, vanilla, sugar and eggs in large bowl. Mix well. Add mincemeat and flour mixture gradually while beating. Add raisins and nuts. Drop by teaspoon onto greased cookie sheet. Bake at 350 degrees for 12 minutes.

*See reference page 307

flaky, tasty pie crust mix

Shared by Noquochoke Orchards, Westport, Massachusetts

1¾ cups shortening	1 egg, well beaten
4 cups flour	½ cup cold water
1 tablespoon sugar	1 tablespoon vinegar
2 teaspoons salt	

INSTRUCTIONS:

Cut in shortening to dry ingredients until crumbly. Slowly add wet ingredients. Makes enough dough for 3 pies with top and bottom crusts.

chocolate banana bread

Shared by Mary Dangelo, Narragansett, Rhode Island

---

²/₃ cup butter

³/₄ cup superfine sugar

2 eggs

2 tablespoons milk

2 ripe bananas, thickly sliced

1 cup self-rising flour

1 tablespoon baking soda

¹/₄ cup Dutch process cocoa powder

¹/₂ cup chocolate chips

INSTRUCTIONS:

Preheat oven to 350 degrees. Grease and flour loaf pan. Cream butter and sugar until pale. Beat in eggs, milk and sliced bananas. Sift in dry ingredients to combine. Lastly, stir in chocolate chips and spoon into loaf pan. Bake for 45 minutes or until skewer comes out clean.

dark chocolate brownies
with coffee caramel and goat cheese swirl

Shared by Fat Toad Farm, Brookfield, Vermont

There is a lady who approaches us on a regular basis at the farmers' market. She is always gushing over how excellent our caramel is swirled into brownies. So, we finally came up with our own brownie recipe using our caramel. To add even more character to the brownies, we add our fresh goat chèvre.

BROWNIES:

8	tablespoons unsalted butter	1	cup sugar
2	ounces unsweetened chocolate	2	teaspoons vanilla
		3	eggs
4	ounces bittersweet chocolate	²/₃	cup all purpose flour
		¹/₄	teaspoon salt
		¹/₂	teaspoon baking powder

FILLING:

1¹/₂	cups plain chèvre*	¹/₂	teaspoon vanilla
¹/₄	cup sugar	1	egg yolk

CARAMEL SWIRL:

4–6	ounces goat milk caramel*	vanilla bean or coffee bean caramel* are other options

INSTRUCTIONS:

Preheat oven to 325 degrees. Grease 8 x 8 pan. To make brownies, melt butter and chopped up chocolate in double broiler. Heat until melted and combined. Take off of heat and add sugar and vanilla. Let cool slightly. Whisk in eggs 1 at a time. Whisk dry ingredients together and combine with wet ingredients until fully incorporated. Set aside.

Cream together all goat cheese filling ingredients.

Pour half the batter into bottom of pan. Using a spoon, drop half the goat cheese filling on top of batter then pour on the remaining batter. Drop the rest of the goat cheese filling on top and swirl with a knife. Drizzle caramel on top. Bake for 50–60 minutes. *See reference page 307*

swedish creme

Shared by Denise Butcher, Ship's Knees Inn,
East Orleans, Massachusetts

Ship's Knees Inn is located less than five minutes from Nauset
Beach in Cape Cod; the perfect getaway for a memorable vacation.
This Inn is filled with character and charm, a must stay!

1 pint whipping cream	1 pint vanilla yogurt
1 cup sugar	frozen raspberries
1 package unflavored	with juice
gelatin	fresh mint leaves
2 teaspoons almond extract	

INSTRUCTIONS:

Make this a day ahead. Mix whipping cream, sugar and gelatin and heat to
steaming point to dissolve sugar; do not boil. Cool for 10–15 minutes,
then add almond extract and yogurt, whisking together slowly. Pour into
small cups and fill two thirds of the way. Just before serving top with
thawed raspberries with juice and fresh mint.

mother's lemon sherbert

Shared by Dinny Wank, Sangerville, Maine

3–4	lemons, juiced	1	pint all purpose cream
1	cup sugar	3	tablespoons sugar
2	cups whole milk	2	teaspoons vanilla

INSTRUCTIONS:

Mix the first 3 ingredients together thoroughly. Pour into a 9 x 13 Pyrex dish. Freeze to firm slush. Whip cream with sugar and vanilla. Add slush, which has been cut into chunks. Continue beating cream mixture until smooth. Pour back in Pyrex dish, cover tightly with foil and freeze. Keeps very well for several weeks in freezer.

di's blueberry pie

Shared by Diane Gardner, Madison, Connecticut

3/4	heaping cup sugar	2	teaspoons freshly squeezed lemon juice
2	tablespoons cornstarch sprinkle cinnamon	2	Pillsbury roll out pie crusts
1/2	cup water		extra sugar, for topping crust
3–3 1/2	cups fresh or frozen blueberries		

INSTRUCTIONS:

Preheat oven to 425 degrees. Spray pie dish with Pam and line with unbaked pie crust.

Meanwhile, combine sugar, cornstarch, cinnamon and water. Heat to a rapid boil until mixture thickens. Set aside and cool for a few minutes, then add blueberries and lemon. Stir together and pour into pie crust.

Take second pie crust and top the pie. Pinch the sides together all around the pie. Cut vents and make a design in the crust. Sprinkle generously with sugar and bake for 20 minutes at 425 degrees. Reduce to 325 and bake for another 20–25 minutes until golden brown.

Serve with vanilla ice cream.

maple glazed pears
with raspberry sauce

*Shared by Jackie Arbuckle, May Farm Bed and Breakfast,
Stowe, Vermont*

**¹/₃ cup fresh or frozen
raspberries, with a
teaspoon of sugar added**

**4 ripe Bosc pears,
with stems**

**¹/₄ cup Vermont maple syrup
cinnamon
light brown sugar**

INSTRUCTIONS:

In a small microwave safe dish, microwave raspberries for about 45 seconds or until soft. Mash the berries thoroughly with a spoon and set aside.

Next, peel the pears, leaving the stems intact. Slice a small piece off the bottom of each pear to help them stand up. Core the pears from the bottom with a corer or melon baller. Stand all the pears together in a Pyrex baking dish. Drizzle maple syrup over each pear until coated. Sprinkle each pear all over with a little cinnamon. Using fingers, pat brown sugar all over each pear. Depending on how juicy the pears are, the sauce can vary from very liquid to almost toffee-like... it doesn't matter.

Cover the baking dish tightly with plastic wrap, leaving it long enough to tuck under the bottom of the dish. This is a crucial step, the dish must be covered tightly so the wrap stays in place. Microwave for about 9–10 minutes, depending on how ripe the pears are. Serve with raspberries.

shortcake biscuits

Shared by Kate Walston, Guilford, Connecticut

I have been making this recipe since my freshman year at Guilford High School. A culinary student spoke about cooking as a profession. Since then I was hooked on the idea of going to culinary school, and I use this recipe whenever I can.

$2\frac{1}{2}$	cups all purpose flour	$\frac{1}{2}$	egg
$\frac{1}{2}$	cup granulated sugar	1	cup heavy cream
1	tablespoon plus $\frac{1}{4}$ teaspoon baking powder	1	tablespoon buttermilk
$\frac{1}{2}$	teaspoon salt	$\frac{1}{2}$	teaspoon vanilla
3	tablespoons unsalted butter, softened	$\frac{1}{4}$	teaspoon lemon juice

INSTRUCTIONS:

Combine flour, sugar, baking powder and salt. Mix together; cut in softened butter until mixed well. Mix together wet ingredients in separate bowl. Make a well in the dry ingredients, add the wet ingredients to the dry in 3 stages, mixing just until combined. If batter is too dry, add a little more heavy cream.

Scoop batter onto greased or papered sheet pan, egg wash the tops of the biscuits and sprinkle with granulated sugar.

Bake at 425 degrees for about 15 minutes or until tops are browned and center is firm. Makes 8 biscuits.

fresh apple pound cake

Shared by Christopher's by the Bay Bed and Breakfast,
Provincetown, Massachusetts

1	cup Wesson oil	3	teaspoons cinnamon
2	cups sugar	1	cup coconut
3	eggs	1	cup black walnuts, chopped
3	cups flour		
1	teaspoon baking soda	3	cups apples, peeled and chopped
1	teaspoon salt		

INSTRUCTIONS:

Beat together oil and sugar. Add 1 egg at a time and mix. Combine remaining ingredients and add to oil mixture. Grease and flour bottom of tube pan and line with parchment paper. Bake at 350 degrees for 1½ hours. Freezes well.

chocolate applesauce cake

Shared by Noquochoke Orchards, Westport, Massachusetts

This cake is over 100 years old! It was my
husband George's grandmother's recipe.

½	cup shortening	½	teaspoon cinnamon
1	cup sugar	½	teaspoon cloves
1½	teaspoons baking soda	½	teaspoon nutmeg
1½	cups applesauce	½	teaspoon allspice
2	cups flour, sifted		nuts, optional
2	tablespoons cocoa		raisins, optional
¼	teaspoon salt		

INSTRUCTIONS:

Grease and flour loaf pan. Cream shortening and sugar, then add baking soda and applesauce to mixture. Mix in flour, cocoa and spices and beat well. Bake at 350 degrees for 50–60 minutes or until toothpick comes out dry. Doubling the recipe makes 7 miniature loaves.

pumpkin pie cake

Shared by Kim Kezer, Amesbury, Massachusetts

This is a very weird recipe to make
but loved by anyone who enjoys pumpkin.

1	14-ounce can pumpkin puree	1	tablespoon pumpkin spice
2	eggs	1/2	teaspoon salt
1 1/2	cups evaporated milk	1	package yellow cake mix
1 1/3	cups granulated sugar	1 1/4	cups pecans, chopped
		1	cup butter, melted

INSTRUCTIONS:

Preheat oven to 350 degrees. Grease 13 x 9 cake pan. Combine pumpkin, eggs, milk, sugar, spice and salt until smoothly blended.

Pour into prepared pan. Sprinkle dry cake mix evenly on top. Scatter nuts over cake mix. Drizzle melted butter over nuts, moistening dry mixture as much as possible. Bake 50–60 minutes or until set and golden. Cool at least 1 hour in the pan on a wire rack before serving. Serve with whipped cream. If there is any leftover, store in the refrigerator.

lemon yogurt cake

Shared by Coffee's Country Market, Old Lyme, Connecticut

CAKE:

1 1/2	cups all purpose flour	3	large eggs
2	teaspoons baking powder	1/4	cup fresh lemon juice
1/2	teaspoon salt	3	teaspoons lemon zest
1	cup plain whole milk yogurt	1/2	teaspoon pure vanilla extract
1	cup sugar	1/2	cup vegetable oil

GLAZE:

1	cup confectioners' sugar	2	tablespoons lemon juice

INSTRUCTIONS:

Preheat oven to 350 degrees. Coat a loaf or bundt pan with butter and flour. Sift flour, baking powder and salt. In another bowl, whisk together the yogurt, sugar, eggs, lemon juice, lemon zest and vanilla. Gently whisk the dry and wet ingredients together. Fold in vegetable oil, making sure all is incorporated. Pour into loaf pan. Bake for 40–50 minutes or until done. Allow it to cool, remove from pan. For the glaze, combine the sugar and lemon juice and pour over the cake.

INDEX

C

D

REFERENCES

Black Watch Farms,
Weathersfield, Vermont ....1-802-263-5548 .... www.blackwatchfarm.com

Champlain Orchards,
Shoreham, Vermont..........................1-802-897-2777 .... www.champlainorchards.com

Sanders Fish Market,
Portsmouth, New Hampshire..........................1-603-436-4568 .... www.sandersfish.com

Paradise Farm Sugarhouse,
West Brattleboro, Vermont ....1-802-258-2026 .... www.pfsugarhouse.com

Cornucopia Wine and Cheese Market,
Stratham, New Hampshire ....1-603-772-4447 .... www.cwinecheese.com

Chatham Fish & Lobster Company,
Chatham, Massachusetts..........................1-800-945-0545 .... www.chathamfishandlobster.com

Noquochoke Orchards,
Westport, Massachusetts ....1-508-636-2237 .... www.noqorchards.com

Caseus Fromagerie and Bistro,
New Haven, Connecticut ....1-203-624-3373 .... www.caseusnewhaven.com

Fat Toad Farm,
Brookfield, Vermont ....1-802-279-0098 .... www.fatoadfarm.com

D'Train's Hot Pepper Sauce,
Westbrook, Connecticut ....1-800-305-9199 .... www.dtrainfoods.com

Claire's Country Garden,
Alburgh, Vermont ....1-802-796-4718 .... www.clairescountrygarden.com

Vermont Butter and Cheese Company,
Websterville, Vermont ....1-800-884-6287 .... www.butterandcheese.net

Formaggio Kitchen,
Cambridge, Massachusetts ....1-888-212-3224 .... www.formaggiokitchen.com

La Laiterie @ Farmstead,
Providence, Rhode Island ....1-401-274-7177 .... www.farmsteadinc.com

Acknowledgements

Several decades before this book was ever conceived, a very important person in my life influenced me to become the person that I am today through her love of family and cooking. My Granny, Sybil Anderson, was an excellent cook... no one could whip up a better Sunday Dinner.

My passion for cooking developed at a very young age, watching my Granny in the kitchen as I stood on a stool, stirring my heart out. She would say, "Diane, put a pinch of salt in this, now a pinch of sugar", and that's how I learned to cook. A pinch of this and a pinch of that, or pour a little of this. Nothing ever measured!

My Mom learned from my Granny, as did our entire family. Now my Mom, or "Gamma" teaches my children when she comes to Connecticut. You can bet that our suppers make a quick turn to good ol' southern food the minute Gamma walks into our house.

While Granny was the inspiration behind all my cookbooks, this book in particular would not be in your hands if it weren't for an amazing group of people. These special people shared my enthusiasm and dedication, not to mention their tolerance for my obsession with perfection.

Kate Waltson, a dear friend and a fantastic baker, would go above and beyond what I needed her to do. Every single recipe that she prepared was filled with love and attention to the smallest of detail. Kate worked nearly all the home photo shoots with me, not only baking, but also assisting in the challenges of food styling for photography.

Marie Waltson was the hands and energy behind the scenes of the photo shoots. She opened her home to me, and gave me a fresh new look for shooting! Marie, also a baker, always came with a big smile and an open heart. Her willingness to take on whatever task was needed to make the day go smoothly was priceless.

Chris Brown, the creative force behind the camera, went to the ends of the earth (figuratively speaking) to get "that perfect shot" that I wanted. It didn't matter that he had 40 shots of the same piece of pie. He would take 40 more if I asked him, even though the very first shot was usually his best. An adventurous travel companion, Chris indulged me to journey along the roads less traveled to find the best recipes.

Stephanie Magriz and Tammy Vaz both have an incredible eye for detail and are responsible for the fantastic creative layout that you see throughout this book. A special thanks to Stephanie, who really stepped in and completed the project, complete layout, cover and the dust jacket. Stephanie worked endless hours day and night, putting her final touches to the design of "What's Cooking in New England?".

Joanne Myszkowski has worked side-by-side with me, assisting in the editorial and promotional concepts. She was my constant sounding board and we enjoyed many meetings at a local coffee house. Her favorite expression to me throughout the hectic months leading up to the final manuscript was "Just Breathe!"

Cindi Gardner, my sister-in-law, generously offered her expertise in editing and design, especially when tight deadlines were looming over my head.

And to my very best friends, Heidi and Ross Shepherd, who have unconditionally loved and supported me through this whole project and have always been there for me. I love you both dearly!

Loretta Tallevast is my mom. My mom took on the job of hand-writing and collecting all of my favorite southern recipes that you will find scattered throughout this book. She traveled to Connecticut from South Carolina to bake, cook, and coordinate the million details that go into preparing for a photo shoot. She is without a doubt one of my biggest supporters! My appreciation for her is positively immeasurable, and goes far beyond what she's done for this book!

My husband Bill is my rock, my constant sounding board and my biggest fan. He is always willing to step in after a photo shoot to try each and every recipe that had been prepared!! His finely-tuned palate provided the guidance to select the final recipes.

And of course my children... Jesse, Ty and Halle, whose enthusiasm for assisting me with launching this third book has transformed this endeavor into a true family business. Their computer-savvy skills have been priceless to me.

And finally, the wonderful people that I met throughout my travels in New England that welcomed me with open arms. They shared their stories and their recipes, but what I found even more powerful was their willingness to share their "pride and joy", whether it was a small country store, a working orchard, or a fabulous restaurant!! For that, I thank all of you from the bottom of my heart.

Happy Cooking!

Diane

Halle, Ty and Jesse

I dedicate this book to each of you.....

you continue to amaze me each and every day!

Travel
ADVENTURES

What's Cooking in New England?

Bill's Seafood, Connecticut

Emmett the Bull with his ladies,
Black Watch Farm, Vermont

LOBSTER POUND
RETAIL HOURS
MON-SAT. 8-5
SUN-HOLIDAYS Closed

THE LOBST

Di holding a 35 pound lobster
Sanders Fish Market
New Hampshire

Fat Toad Farm, Vermont

After a long photo shoot in Connecticut

Siasconset Bike Path   Peter Foulger &
Surfside Bike Path   Whaling Museum
Polpis-Wauwinet   Info Bur-Rest Rooms
          Macy-Hadwen &
          Oldest House
          Old Mill-Old Gaol
          Maria Mitchell   Police Station
Hospital-Airport

Lost in Nantucket, Massachusetts